Contents

FOLD and DO

52 pencil-popping, wiggle-stopping things to do in Church

Carla Williams

Illustrated By Richard M. Heroldt

CPH
SAINT LOUIS

Introduction

Waiting, whether it be sitting in church or in the doctor's office can be tedious—especially for children. *Fold and Do* offers Bible-centered activities for children to do during these times.

The 52 lessons in *Fold and Do* provide ideas that pertain to church life, spiritual disciplines, and holidays. The reproducible pages are easily folded in half to slip inside church bulletins, a purse, or a backpack. Each handout provides three to four activities that children can quietly do while sitting in a church pew, riding in the car, waiting for Sunday school to begin, or as part of family devotions. Themes or holidays can be selected to correspond with the appointed Scripture readings for a Sunday or for selected lessons in the classroom.

Each two-sided sheet in *Fold and Do* includes a memory verse, Scripture search, problem-solving activities, and an application. There is no need for crayons, scissors, or messy glue—just a pen or pencil and a New International Version Bible.

The blank box printed on each sheet provides a space for churches or Sunday school teachers to add their own announcements. If used at home, parents can write a personal note in these boxes.

It is my prayer that these activities will draw the children in your life closer to God.

Carla Williams

How to Use This Book

1. Select the lesson(s) you will use.

2. Make two-sided photocopies of the lesson, one per child.

3. Fold the lesson in half.

4. Make available for children to do.

Come to the House of the Lord

God's family gathers to hear and tell of God's wonderful love. This time together is called *worship*. Shade in each space that has a numeral in it to discover a place where God's family gathers.

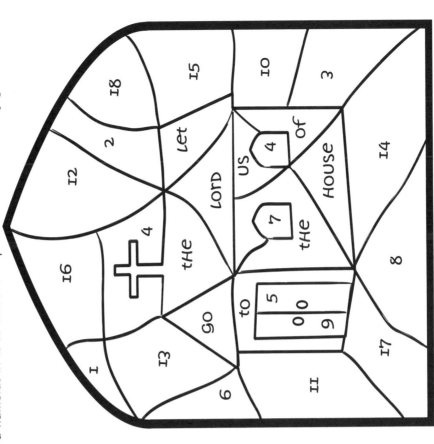

Arrange the words to find the Bible words hidden in the stained glass window.

_____

_____ (Psalm 122:1b).

Make a list of things you learned from today's lesson or church sermon.

1. _____

2. _____

3. _____

Now draw a star next to the one thing you want to remember and do this week.

Things We Do At Church

Unscramble these words that tell some of the things we do at church. In each box draw a picture of the word.

1. gins
_ _ _ _

2. vegi
_ _ _ _

3. rayp
_ _ _ _

4. netisl
_ _ _ _ _ _

5. eard het leBib
_ _ _ _   _ _ _   _ _ _ _ _

Getting Ready

Were you ready for church this morning? Sometimes families argue and feel unhappy when everyone is in a hurry to get ready. Has your family ever felt that way? Would you like to help? You can plan ahead to be ready for church.

Make a list of things you could do that might help your family get ready for church. Here are some ideas to get you started.

Getting Ready:

+ Lay out your clothes.

+ _____

+ _____

+ _____

+ _____

Day of Worship:

+ Get up on time.

+ _____

+ _____

+ _____

+ _____

+ _____

2

New Year Promises

People like to start the New Year making promises to change or do something special. Sometimes it's hard for us to keep promises. But God always keeps His promises.

Look up the Bible verses.
Match the stories with God's promises.

God promised to ...

send His Son.	**Genesis 9:11–13**
never flood the earth again.	**Deuteronomy 1:21**
take His people into the Promised Land.	**1 John 4:14**

The LORD is faithful to all His promises.
(Psalm 145:13)

Keeping Promises

The LORD is faithful to all His promises (Psalm 145:13).

God keeps all of His promises. Pick one thing from your list of promises on page 2. Draw a picture of the way you will try to keep that promise. Hang it where it will remind you to keep your promise.

Making Promises

Keeping a promise is a good thing to try to do. What could you ask God to help you do better this new year? Here are some ideas:

- Spend more time reading the Bible.
- Help around the house.
- Do homework without being reminded.

Add your own promises.

God Helps Us Keep Promises

Sometimes it's hard to keep promises. We try and try, but forget and break our word. God keeps His promises and He helps us keep ours. Pick one thing from the list you just made and use it to finish this prayer.

Dear God,

Thank You for keeping all Your promises.

Please help me to _____ in this brand new year. In Jesus' name. Amen.

Rainbows remind us that God keeps His promises. Inside the rainbow, write some words that will help you remember to try to keep the promise you prayed about.

Ask for help

Sing to the Lord

In worship we listen to God, we talk to God. In response to His words of love for us, we sing His praises.

Words have been hidden inside another mixed-up word. Use the clue to find the hidden word. Write the word on the blanks.

(something just made)
S X N T Y E U W ___ ___ ___

(making musical sounds with words)
M A S B I K N L G ___ ___ ___

(music and words for singing)
S P M O W N G T ___ ___ ___

(everything)
B A S L W L T Q Z ___ ___ ___

(God is ...)
Y A L T O O Q R P D ___ ___ ___

(the world)
H E U A R G T N H ___ ___ ___

Use the words you found to fill in the blanks in the Bible verse. Some words will be used twice.

___ ___ to the ___ a ___ ___;
___ ___ to the ___ ___, ___ ___
the ___ ___. (Psalm 96:1)

Sing a New Song

If you could write a song telling of your love for God, what would you say? Write the words to your song in the space below.

If you want, teach your song to a friend.

What is your favorite song or hymn? Does it make you think of heaven, or Jesus on the cross, or God's love? Draw a picture showing what your favorite song makes you think about.

Musical Instruments

The Bible tells us to praise the Lord with musical instruments. Look up each Bible verse and draw a line to that instrument. Some verses may have more than one instrument.

Matthew 24:31

Psalm 150:5

Daniel 3:5

1 Samuel 16:16

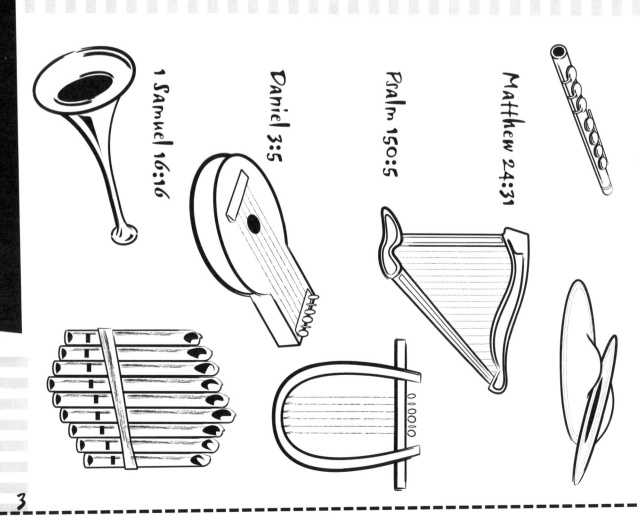

I Can Give to the Church

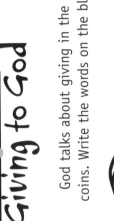

Find and circle the hidden words in the box below. The pictures give you clues to the words. Each picture represents one way you can give to your church.

I can give my ...

A	T	I	M	E	X	M
P	O	Q	L	U	E	O
L	O	V	E	N	I	N
E	A	T	X	V	B	E
H	W	I	P	R	A	Y
T	S	D	F	V	G	B

4

Giving to God

God talks about giving in the Bible. Unscramble the words in the coins. Write the words on the blanks below.

_____ _____ _____ _____ (2 Corinthians 9:7).

A Cheerful Giver

Mark 12:41-44 tells of a woman who gave all she had to God. She was a cheerful giver. Read the story and find the answers to this puzzle.

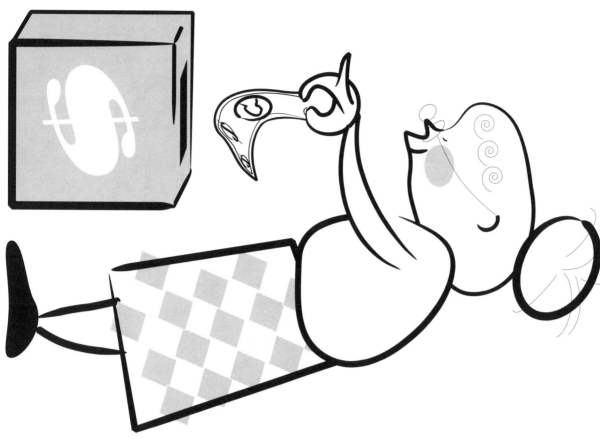

Across

2. The woman was a _____.
4. Jesus sat in the _____.
6. The woman was very _____.
8. The two coins were worth less than a _____.
10. Jesus watches as people put money into the temple _____.
12. The crowd was rich and had lots of _____.

Down

2. Most of the people gave out of their _____.
3. Jesus called His _____.
5. The widow put in _____ she had.
7. The crowd gave out of their riches but the woman gave out of her _____.
9. The widow put in two _____ coins.
11. Money given to the temple was called an _____.

4

5 God Made Me Special

God had a special plan in mind when He created you. Isn't that wonderful? David (the shepherd boy who became king) trusted that God had a plan for him. Work this rebus to find out what he said.

 – y + ise   u

  – e +  – t + use

 – h   f + 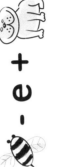 + _E ly

and 1 (spelled with a w) + der + _E ly

 – y + de.   Psalm 139:14

Made for a Special Purpose

You were wonderfully made by God. He made you for a special purpose and He gave you special skills. Maybe you are a creative writer, or a beautiful singer, or a good friend. Write about or draw a picture of one thing God made special about you. How can you use this to show God that you love Him?

Name That Body Part

God made each part of your body with its own job. Look up these Bible verses to discover what body part is described in each verse:

The lamp of the body (Matthew 6:22). _____

Stands on level ground (Psalm 26:12). _____

This part is a fire (James 3:6). _____

Once used as a pencil in the Bible (Daniel 5:5). _____

Now read these riddles and name the parts of the body.

You can use us to praise and clap,
But please don't use us to hurt or slap.

Each of us has five friends that wiggle,
And poke your sides to make you giggle.

Jesus had some, where nails were driven,
To show us that our sins are forgiven.

What are we?

_____

We use this part
To eat our food,
And everything
That tastes good.

And from it sweet
Words can flow,
Or phrases that
Hurt others so.

But we open it wide,
And sing God's praise.
And to Him
Let our voices raise.

What is it?

_____

To show us how to love one another,
Jesus washed the _____ of His brother.

5

6

Valentine Love

Read the words on the hearts. Cross out all of the hearts that have words that do not show what love is. Then fill in the blanks to complete the Bible verse.

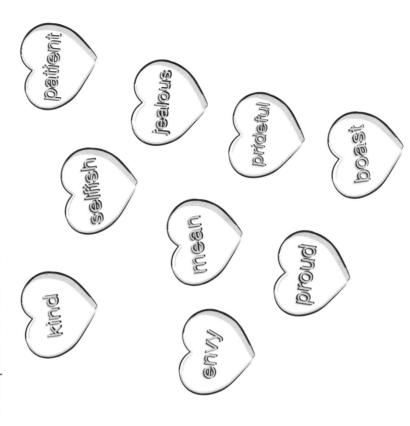

patient
jealous
selfish
prideful
boast
kind
mean
envy
proud

Love is __ __ __ __ __ __ t, love is __ i __ __ __ .

It does not __ __ __ __ v __ , it does not __ __ __ s __ ,

it is not __ __ __ __ u __ (1 Corinthians 13:4).

Love One Another

In Mark 12:30–31 Jesus shares two of God's greatest commandments. To learn what they are, start at the arrow and follow the path around the heart.

LOVE GOD WITH ALL YOUR HEART
LOVE YOUR NEIGHBOR AS YOURSELF

Draw arrows from the words that remind you to love God to "God," and from the ones that remind you to love your neighbor to "Neighbor." (Some words can have two arrows.)

GOD

NEIGHBOR

obey
share
worship
help
pray
kindness

Valentine was a man who lived long ago. Legend tells us that his love for God was so great he was willing to die for his faith. His name was given to a celebration we now call St. Valentine's Day.

Put an **x** on the blanks that describe ways to show God that you love Him. Cross out those that do _not_ show you love God.

_____ Tell others about Jesus.

_____ Don't share with others.

_____ Read the Bible every day.

_____ Talk about God at school.

_____ Cheat on your homework.

_____ Pray for your friends.

Can you list some other ways to show that you love God?

_____

_____

_____

_____

Valentine

Read each Bible verse. If it speaks of love, draw a heart. If it does not, mark an **x**.

1 Corinthians 13:1

Jude:2

Psalm 6:9

John 3:16

1 John 2:10

1 Thessalonians 3:12

Which one of these Bible verses would you like to share with someone you love? Write out the verse.

_____

_____

_____

_____

Leadership

In the Old Testament, the people had no leaders. They were often confused. God appointed leaders to help guide the people. Soon God chose kings to rule the people. The New Testament tells us that God is in control and wants us to honor and obey our leaders.

Are you a leader of a group? Put an ✘ by the things you could do to be a good leader. If you are not a leader, then put a check-mark ✔ by the ways you can honor your leaders.

___ Listen to other's ideas.

___ Pray for the leaders.

___ Help others.

___ Obey the rules.

___ Encourage each person to share.

___ Show respect.

___ Take a stand for what is right.

7

Honor Our Leaders

Rules are needed when people live and work together. Leaders are chosen who decide the rules. A government is when leaders work together to make laws for the people so that everyone is treated fairly and justly. Look at the words in the circles. Use the clues to figure out where each word belongs.

submit

Himself

governing

must

to

authorities

Everyone

the

1. Has a number word in it. _ _ _ _

2. Begins with m and ends with t.   m _ _ _ t

3. Starts with the word "sub."   sub _ _ _

4. It is made up of two smaller words. _ _ _ _ _ _ _

5. Begins with t and ends with o. _ _

6. Begins and ends with the same letter. _ _ _

7. Its beginning and ending letters spell as. a _ _ _ _ _ _ _ _ _ s

Put the words together to make the Bible verse.

_____

_____ (Romans 13:1).

Leaders in the Bible

God commanded that we obey our leaders. Look up the verses below each name. Draw a line between the people who obeyed and the leader they obeyed.

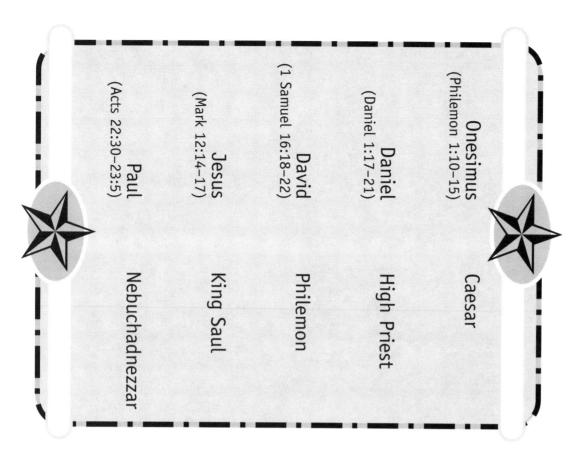

Onesimus
(Philemon 1:10–15)

Daniel
(Daniel 1:17–21)

David
(1 Samuel 16:18–22)

Jesus
(Mark 12:14–17)

Paul
(Acts 22:30–23:5)

Caesar

High Priest

Philemon

King Saul

Nebuchadnezzar

Honoring and Obeying Authority

Romans 13:1 tells us that God has established every authority. We honor authorities by obeying the rules they set down. Put a ☺ by the ways we can obey authority. Put a ☹ by the ways that show disrespect.

_____ Obey traffic laws while riding your bike.

_____ Steal a candy bar from the store.

_____ Follow the school rules.

_____ Take out the trash.

_____ Cheat on a test at school.

_____ Help straighten chairs in Sunday school.

God gave us governing authorities to help us. It is important to pray for our leaders. Place a coin "heads up" under this part of the page. Rub it with a pencil or pen to see someone that we honor and remember.

Talking to God

Jesus came to be our Savior. One day the disciples asked Jesus to teach them to do something special. Follow the maze to find out what they wanted to learn from Jesus.

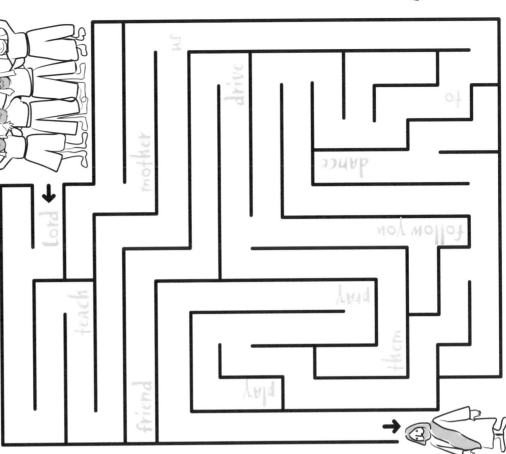

Lord • mother • drive • in • dance • to • teach • pray • follow you • friend • play • them

Luke 11:1

In Your Own Words

Read Matthew 6:9–13 to find out how Jesus told His disciples to pray. Then write a prayer using the following words.

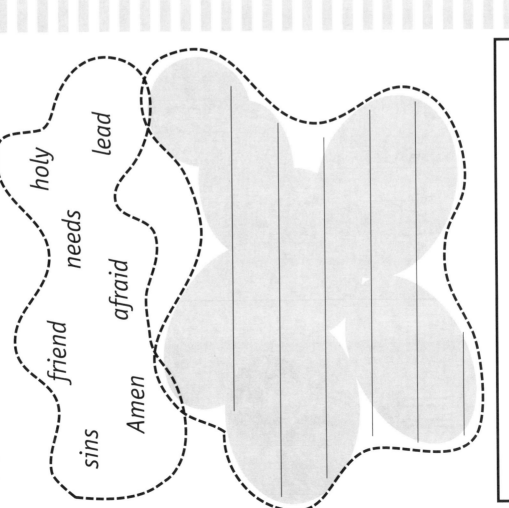

holy • lead • friend • needs • afraid • sins • Amen

People Who Talked to God

Look up the Bible verses and draw a line from the name of each person to what they talked to God about.

Hannah
(1 Samuel 1:10–11)

Solomon
(1 Kings 8:27–29)

Jesus
(Mark 6:41)

Jonah
(Jonah 1:16–2:10)

Talking with Friends

Jesus is our Savior and He calls us His friends. You can talk to Him just like you do any friend. Below are some pictures of things you can talk to God about. Circle the ones you would like to pray about today.

The Parables of Jesus

Jesus taught His disciples using a type of story called a *parable*. Each parable was a lesson. He used examples that would help listeners learn more about God and His love.

Look at the pictures and see who else teaches you lessons. Fill in the blanks.

T _ _ _ r

P _ _ t _ _ _

M _ _ _ and _ _ a _

He taught them many things by parables (Mark 4:2).

Teaching Others

What is your favorite parable? What lesson did you learn from it?

If you could teach a friend one lesson from the parables, what would it be? Draw a picture of the story you would like to tell.

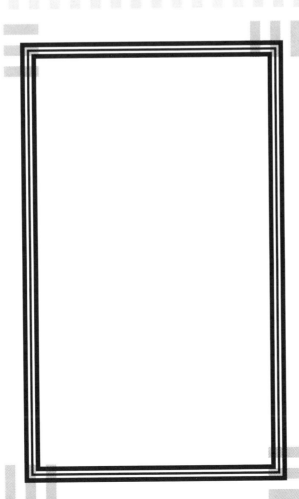

Now write a few sentences telling the lesson.

Lessons to Learn

Jesus' parables always have a lesson for us to learn. Use the words listed below to fill in the blanks that give the true meaning of each parable.

TRUST

FAITH

FORGIVENESS

JESUS

The tiny mustard seed teaches that we only need a little _____. (Matthew 17:20)

The prodigal son found _____ from his father. (Luke 15:11—23)

The wise man teaches us to _____ Jesus. (Matthew 7:24—29)

The lost sheep know that _____ is the Good Shepherd. (Luke 15:3—7)

What's Your Favorite Parable?

Look up these Bible verses to read some of the parables. Use the clue on the line to write a key word from that parable. The first one has been done for you.

Matthew 13:45—46 Ⓟ PEARL

Matthew 25:1—13 Ⓐ _____

Luke 16:19—31 Ⓡ _____

Matthew 7:24—27 Ⓐ _____

Luke 14:16 Ⓑ _____

Matthew 25:14—30 Ⓛ _____

Matthew 13:31 Ⓔ _____

Matthew 18:12—14 Ⓢ _____

The Holy Trinity

Therefore go and make disciples of all nations, baptizing them in the name of the Father and of the Son and of the Holy Spirit (Matthew 28:19).

Hundreds of years ago a young man named Patrick traveled the countryside telling people about God.

One day he stood before the king of Ireland. Patrick wanted to teach the king that God was three Persons in one. So he plucked a shamrock and showed it to the king. He explained that the shamrock was one leaf made up of three leaflets. He told the king that God was three Persons—Father, Son, and Holy Spirit—but still one God.

Now the shamrock is often used to remind us that God is the Holy Trinity. Write names of the three Persons of God on the shamrock.

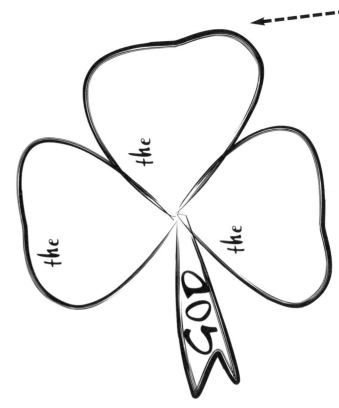

Three-in-One

God the *Father* made us and protects us. Jesus the *Son* gave His life for the forgiveness of our sins. The *Holy Spirit* gives us faith. Think of some words for *Father, Son,* and *Holy Spirit* and write them in the leaflets of the shamrock.

If you need some help look up these verses: Psalm 19:1, 1 John 3:7, Romans 6:4, and Psalm 22:28.

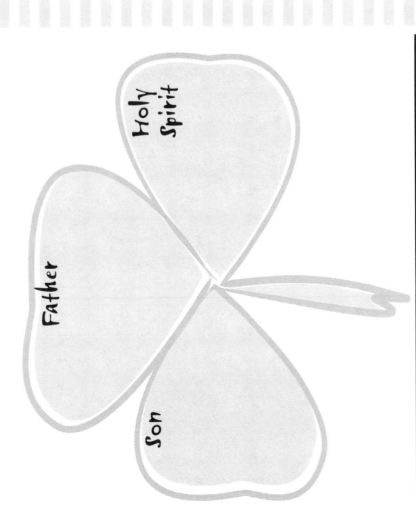

One True God

St. Patrick's Day can help us remember that God is Three-in-One. Inside each circle are hidden letters. Find the letters that spell out the name for Three-in-One.

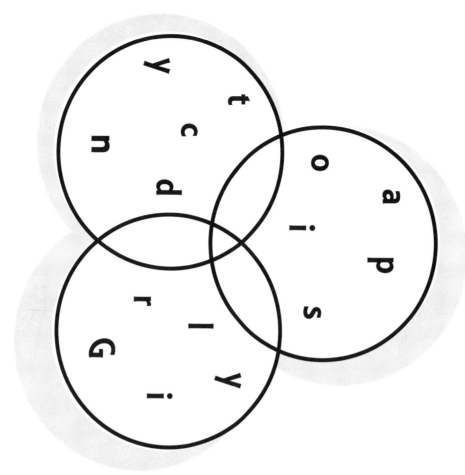

H _ _ _ T _ _ _ _ _

Names of God

The prophet Isaiah foretold that Jesus would have many names. These names tell about the three Persons of God.

For to us a child is born, to us a Son is given, and the government will be on His shoulders. And He will be called Wonderful Counselor, Mighty God, Everlasting Father, Prince of Peace (Isaiah 9:6).

Find and circle all the names for Jesus. (Clue: They are underlined in the Bible verse above.)

```
W C T V T F C S R C S L Z Z Y T E
B O X I L P Q C L A N J E N D M J V
M Q N W P W P C Z W Q F E X U G U E
W S G D T M M B D E K X D S C V L R
U B P Q E G C R Y T J S L W N Y B L
H X E G C R M U N Q M P A R M R A T
P N L T Q W F G O X P R E E T P U S
W N D A S D I U S U I Y H X L Y W T
O I V R E Z O B L N U O S I V H Z I
E O N G T A G C C Y H P R T X Z N H
A W O B M H O M D T V U L J P J H F
U R E C G F C Y F Y H G N B B X B A
T I R I P S Y L O H W G H S M N B T
H Z X E P U K D Q W U F I U E F M H
H S A N S K U C T E E B S M C L D E
G C F O K Z V T B L C D Q X P Z O R
E B V L E P E T H H J S Y B D O J R
```

The Peace of God

Do you ever worry? Do things ever scare you? We all have fears, but we do not need to be troubled because God has the perfect answer for us.

Do these math problems. Use the code to find the letter each number stands for. Then write the letters in the blanks below each column. Read the sentence to learn God's help for us when we are troubled.

2 + 1 = 3   3 + 3 = ___   5 + 5 = ___

4 + 4 = ___   7 + 2 = ___   9 - 4 = ___

6 + 8 = ___   8 + 9 = ___

10 - 1 = ___   8 - 3 = ___   ___ ___

6 + 9 = ___   7 + 8 = ___   10 + 3 = ___

8 + 8 = ___   4 + 1 = ___

___ ___ ___ ___   6 - 5 = ___

C ___ ___ ___ ___   7 - 4 = ___

                              8 - 3 = ___

                              ___ ___ ___ ___ ___

key

1=a 2=b 3=c 4=d 5=e 6=g 7=f
8=h 9=l 10=m 11=n 12=o 13=p
14=r 15=s 16=t 17=v

Peace I leave with you; My peace I give you ... Do not let your hearts be troubled and do not be afraid (John 14:27).

Peace in Your Heart

No matter what happens, God can bring peace to your heart. Inside the heart, draw a picture of one thing that scares you. Ask God to give you His peace.

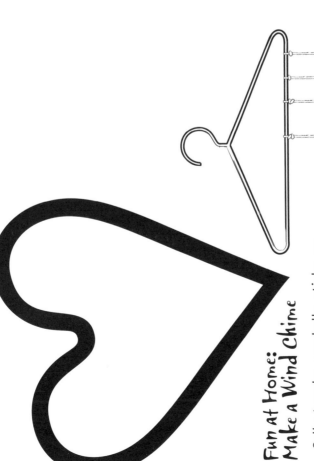

Fun at Home:
Make a Wind Chime

Collect rocks, seashells, sticks, or nails. Tie them on strings and hang from a clothes hanger to make a wind chime. Hang where the wind will move it to help you remember that Jesus calmed the storm.

Jesus Calms the Storm

Read the story in Mark 4:36–41 to find out how Jesus brought peace in the middle of a storm. Number the pictures in the order they happened in the story.

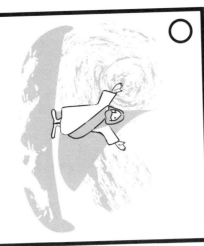

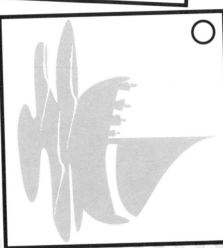

God Gives Us Peace

Sometimes troubles or storms blow in our lives. Figure out each rhyme to find out what gives you peace in these times. Look up the Bible verses if you need help.

When you are afraid
of the dark night,
The Word of God will be
your _____.
(Psalm 119:105)

If you give a speech
and feel really weak,
Pray to God to give
you words to _____.
(Exodus 4:12)

In the middle of a windy storm,
Jesus keeps you safe and _____.
(Luke 8:24)

12

Springtime

It's spring! Unscramble the words in each part of the flower. Then put the words in order. What do you think this Bible verse says about spring?

EH HVGERNETI METI EADM SAH NI EBFAULFIU STI

b _ _ _ _ _ _ _ _ m _ _ _ _ e _ _ _ _ m _ _.

(Ecclesiastes 3:11a)

Changes

With God's help, Jonah changed his mind. God also helps you change. Look up the verses. Draw a line to the picture that shows the changes God can help you make.

Ephesians 6:1

1 Corinthians 4:12

Psalm 146:7

Romans 12:13

Beautiful Words

Springtime reminds us that God makes all things beautiful. How many different words can you make using the letters in the word **beautiful?**

———— ———— ————

———— ———— ————

———— ———— ————

———— ———— ————

Draw a picture showing something God has made beautiful in your own life.

Change of Heart

Spring brings changes ... changes in the weather, changes in nature, changes in our activities, changes in what we wear.

Sometimes we need changes in our life too. Read Jonah 1–2:2 and 3:1–3 to find out how Jonah had a change of heart. Lead Jonah to Nineveh. Stop along the way stop to see what happened.

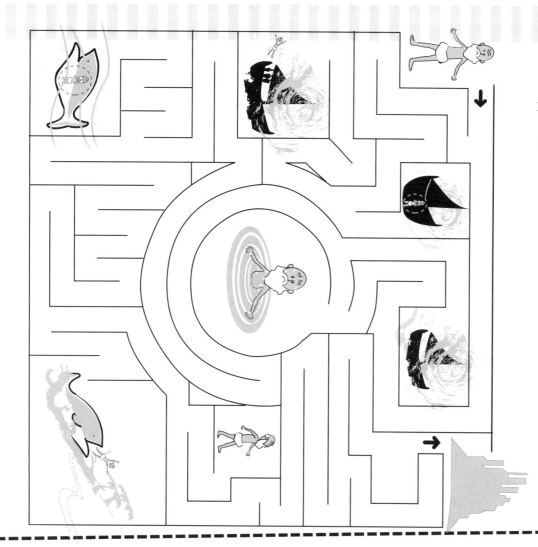

13

John the Baptist

John the Baptist lived in the wilderness. He wore camel skin and ate honey and locusts. As John traveled through the land, he had a special message for those who came to hear him. Use the code to fill in the letters to find John's message.

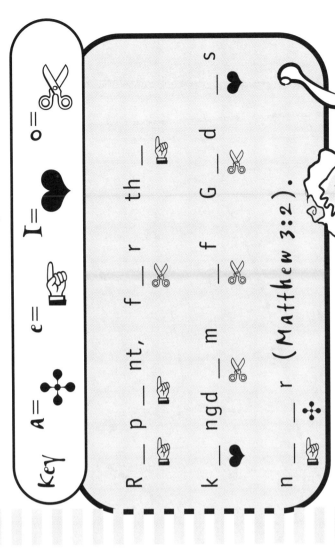

key A= ♣ e= ☝ I= ♥ o= ✂

R_p_nt, f_r th_ ☝

k_ngd_m _f G_d

n__r (Matthew 3:2).

We Come to God

Use these words to fill in the blanks below:

PLEASED   CHILDREN   SINS   SPIRIT   SCRIPTURE

Jesus fulfilled all _ _ _ _ _ _ _ _ _.
God was _ _ _ _ _ _ _ *with His Son.*
Our _ _ _ _ *are washed away.*
When we are baptized we become _ _ _ _ _ _ _ _ *of God.*
God sends His _ _ _ _ _ _ *to work faith in our hearts.*

Now find and circle the same words.

E R K O N C X N Z E U Z
M C X O K G E X T R E Y
Y O N M N R F B I U P A
O M U A D U D H R T L U
C U L T G U W I P E Q
X Y I T Q N K J P I A S
W H C O N F E S S R S U
C S N I S O P P S C E B
B O Q X D I Y O E S D D

© 2001 Carla Williams   Used by permission of Concordia Publishing House

Mystery Shape

Read Matthew 3:1–17. Color all the areas with a Bible verse that uses the words **baptized**, **baptizing**, **repent**, or **repentance**.

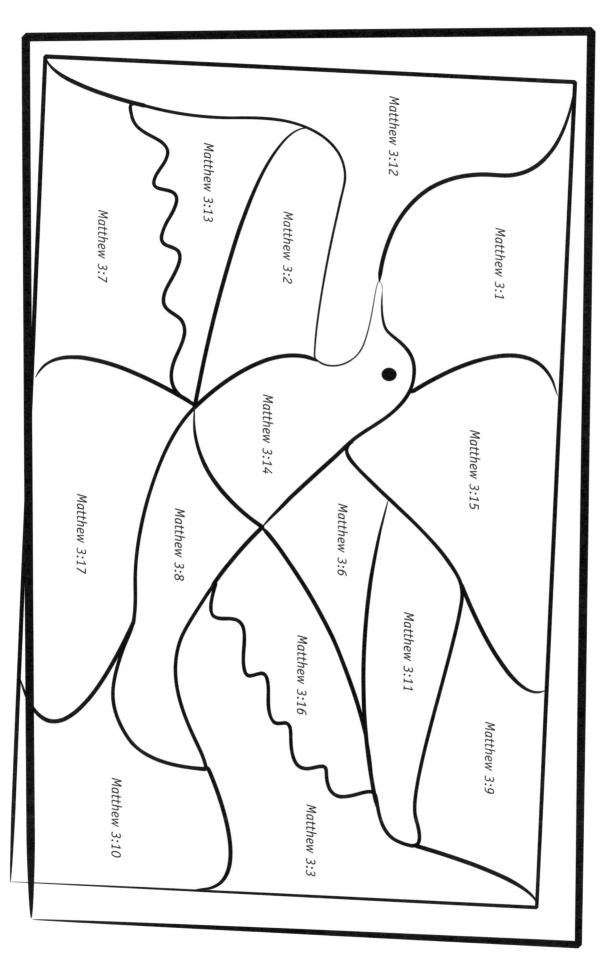

Matthew 3:12

Matthew 3:13

Matthew 3:7

Matthew 3:2

Matthew 3:1

Matthew 3:14

Matthew 3:15

Matthew 3:17

Matthew 3:8

Matthew 3:6

Matthew 3:11

Matthew 3:16

Matthew 3:9

Matthew 3:10

Matthew 3:3

Ash Wednesday

Ash Wednesday is the first day of Lent. It is a time to repent and pray. During Lent, we remember what Jesus did for us. Color all the spaces with circles to reveal what Christ did for the forgiveness of our sins.

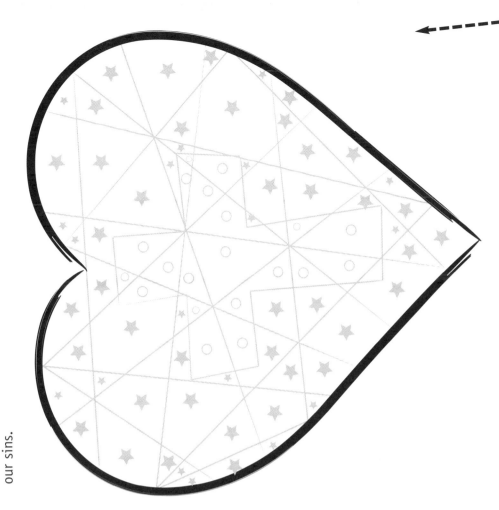

We believe that Jesus died and rose again.
(1 Thessalonians 4:14a)

A Time of Fasting

During Lent we can fast (give up something to eat or do for a short period of time) to help us remember what Christ gave up for us. Circle something you could give up during Lent.

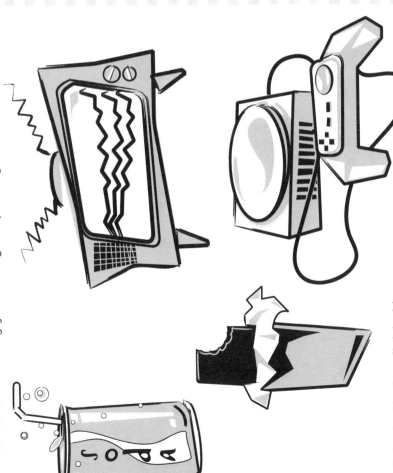

Fill in the blank to finish this prayer.

Dear Jesus,

Thank You for giving Your life for me. Help me as I give up _____ for Lent. I love You, Lord. Thank You for loving me. Amen.

The Sacrificed Lamb

In the Old Testament, people showed that they loved God by sacrificing a lamb. Jesus is called the Lamb of God because God sacrificed His Son for us. Jesus willingly died so our sins could be forgiven.

Use the maze to lead the lamb to the altar.

Death to Life

During Lent we can fast, pray, and repent to show how thankful we are that Jesus died for our sins. The wonderful news is that He rose again!

Connect the dots to find a picture that reminds us that we have new life in Jesus.

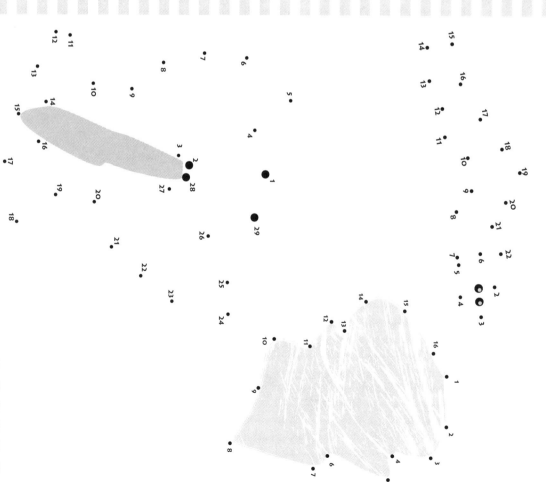

Palm Sunday

On Palm Sunday Jesus rode into Jerusalem. Hidden inside each palm is a word. Put the correct words in the blanks to discover what the excited people shouted.

_ _ _ _ _ _ !

_ _ _ _ _ _ _ _ _ !

(Mark 11:9)

name
the
comes
is
Hosanna
of
the
he
who
in
Lord
Blessed

Praising the Son of God

Use the code to discover ways you can praise the Lord this week.

Key   A   E   I   O   U   Y

C L _ P P _ N G

S _ N G _ N G

R _ J _ _ C _ N G

W _ R SH _ P _ N G

Can you think of any other ways to praise Jesus?

© 2001 Carla Williams   Used by permission of Concordia Publishing House

One way to praise the Lord is with music and song. Hidden in the picture are 2 trumpets, 1 violin, 3 harps, 2 saxophones, 4 guitars, and 5 musical notes.

Write the titles of your favorite hymns on the sheets of music.

15

16

The Lord's Supper

In the Lord's Supper we remember Christ's life, death, and resurrection. Draw a picture of what you think about during Holy Communion.

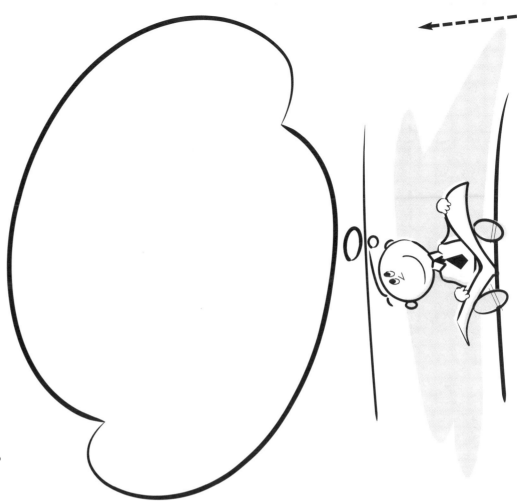

Do this in remembrance of Me (Luke 22:19).

Remember Jesus

Holy Communion helps us remember that Jesus gave His body and blood for the forgiveness of our sins. Look up the Bible verses. Draw a line from each verse to the part of the Lord's Supper it makes you think of.

Matthew 6:11

Luke 9:23

Mark 14:23

John 6:68

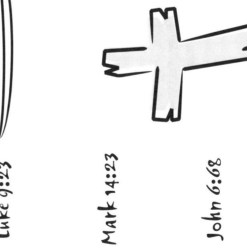

© 2001 Carla Williams   Used by permission of Concordia Publishing House

When we break the bread, we remember that Jesus gave His body as a sacrifice. When we drink the wine, we remember that Jesus shed His blood for us.

During Holy Communion you may hear the following words: **BLOOD, BODY, CUP, BREAD, DRINK, EAT, JESUS, SHED, WINE.**

Find these words in the puzzle.

D	J	Y	T	P	N	D	U
D	R	E	D	A	H	O	P
E	B	I	S	O	E	O	D
H	L	J	N	U	B	L	A
S	T	U	X	K	S	B	E
A	W	I	N	E	T	C	R
D	E	I	D	C	U	P	B

Communion with Christ

The Greek word *koinonia* means communion. Hidden in the picture are the letters that form a word that means *koinonia* or communion.

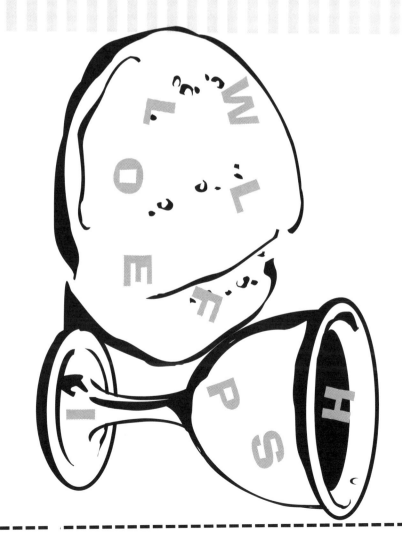

In the Lord's Supper we have

_ _ _ _ _ _ _ with Jesus.

Good News

It is always exciting to hear good news, especially when it comes from God. Use the first letter of each item to discover a message of Good News meant just for you.

Christ died for our sins ... was buried ... [and] raised on the third day (1 Corinthians 15:3).

Go Tell Others

Mary ran to tell the others that Jesus had risen from the dead. Draw a line between each child and someone they could tell about Jesus.

Fill in the blank:

I will tell _____ about Jesus.

The Path to New Life

Trace the path Jesus followed so we might have New Life.

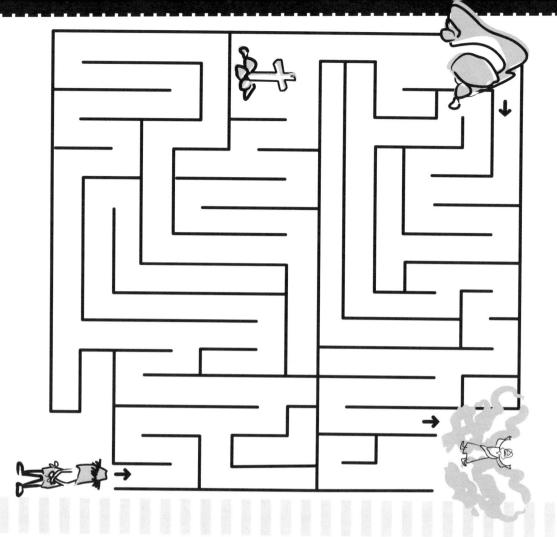

The Empty Tomb

How do you think the friends of Jesus felt when they discovered the tomb was empty? What news made them happy? Write a letter telling the story as if you were there on Easter morning.

Dear _____

Today I went to the tomb of Jesus our Lord.

Praying All Day Long

You can talk to God any time of the day or night. What time of day do you pray to God? Draw hands on the clock at your favorite time to pray.

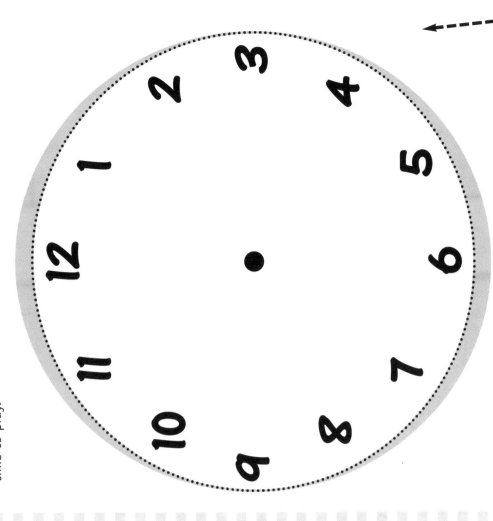

Pray continually (1 Thessalonians 5:17).

I Can Pray Continually

Daniel prayed to God three times every day. Sometimes we get so busy that we forget to pray. Make a pledge to pray at least three times each day. Write *where* you will pray:

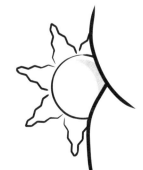

I will pray in the **morning** _____.

I will pray at **noon** _____.

I will pray at **night** _____.

Daniel Prayed

Some men were jealous of Daniel and got him into trouble for praying to God. Read what happened in Daniel 6:3–24.

These pictures tell the story, but they are all mixed up. Number them in the correct order. One can be used twice.

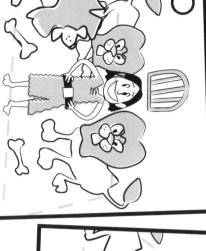

Jesus Prayed

Jesus prayed too. Look up each Bible verse, then fill in the blank. Draw a picture of a time when Jesus prayed.

Jesus went up on a ———— to pray (Matthew 14:23).

Jesus spent the ———— praying (Luke 6:12).

Jesus prayed very early in the ———— (Mark 1:35).

19

A Special Day for Mom

The mother of Anna Jarvis wanted a special day set aside just to honor mothers. Anna talked to many people about this. In 1907, her dream came true when the first Mother's Day was celebrated.

Write H on the first blank. Then go around the heart, skip every other letter, and write those letters on the blanks below.

START HERE

H O R P S O N Q Z R X Y W O B U D R A W C O S T Q H D E P

_ _ _ _ _ _ _ _ _ _ _ . *(Ephesians 6:2)*

Dear Mom

Write a letter to Mom telling how you will honor her.

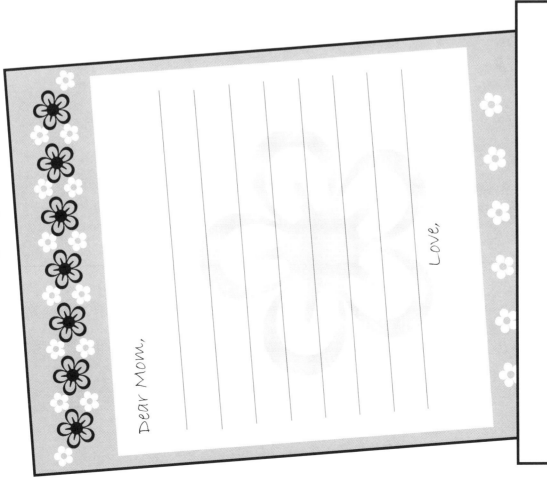

Dear Mom,

Love,

Honor Your Mother Every Day

God wants you to honor your mother, not just today, but every day. Using the picture clues discover ways to show love to your mom.

God's words in the tell me to do what my  asks.

 should to her when she speaks to me.

Helping around the shows that honor my .

Every day can give her a big  and tell her that

 her.

 will remember to  for my  and God will

to my prayers.

My  is a special  from God.

 will h _ _ _ _ _ _ and obey my  .

Bible Mothers

Look up the Bible verses and read all about these mothers. Match the mothers to their children.

Hannah
(1 Samuel 1:1–20)

Sarah
(Genesis 21:1–5)

Eve
(Genesis 4:1–2)

Elizabeth
(Luke 1:5–25)

Mary
(Matthew 1:18–25)

John

Samuel

Cain and
Abel

Jesus

Isaac

Learning to Serve

The Bible tells about many people who gladly served God and others. Samuel happily helped Eli in the temple, Dorcas made clothes for the poor, and Paul eagerly told about Jesus.

Unscramble the words. Then place them in the Bible verse to discover how we too can serve.

(s a)   (v e r S e)   (e t h)   (d o r L)

_____ _____ _____ _____

(o y u)   (h e l e w o d y h l e t r a)

_____ _____

l __ h

(f i)   (n m e)   (r v e n g i s)

_____ _____ _____

(t n o)   (r w e e)

_____ _____

a _____ I _____ r _____ u _____

e _____ o _____ , _____ o _____ m _____ (Ephesians 6:7).

Serve with All Your Heart

Draw a picture of how you want to serve others at home or in your community.

Serve one another in love. (Galatians 5:13)

Working Hard to Serve

There are many ways to serve our Lord. Circle the words below that describe what is happening in the picture.

CHILDREN	MEAN	PLAY
HELP	WORK	
SAD	SERVE	WASH

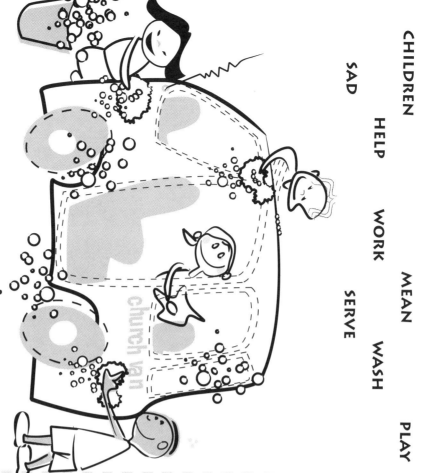

church van

What can you do to serve the Lord?

_____

_____

_____

Serve Joyfully

Pretend you are the child serving in each picture. Think about how would you feel if you ...

Jesus *wants* us to serve *wholeheartedly!* No *matter what!*

A Cloud of Witnesses

Therefore, since we are surrounded by such a great cloud of witnesses, let us throw off ... the sin that so easily entangles, and let us run with perseverance the race marked out for us (Hebrews 12:1).

Help this boy run the race to Jesus. Do you recognize the special people, or witnesses, who are cheering along the way?

My Hero of Faith

A hero is someone whose example you want to follow. The Bible is filled with true stories about people who lived as faithful followers of God. Who is your favorite Bible hero? Write the name of your Bible hero in the pennant below. Then write what you have learned from the example of that person.

MY HERO OF FAITH

WHAT I LEARN FROM MY HERO

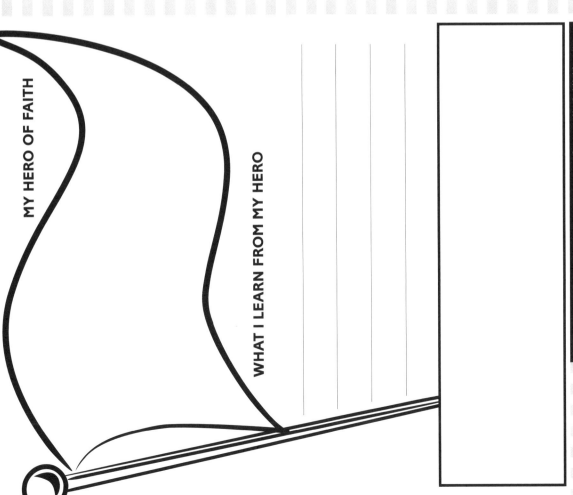

Lessons to Learn

Look up these Old Testament Bible stories. As you read each one, draw a line from that person to the lesson God helps us learn from him or her.

David
(1 Samuel 17:41–50)

Moses
(Deuteronomy 4:13–14)

Hannah
(1 Samuel 1:13–20)

Daniel
(Daniel 6:10–24)

Noah
(Genesis 9:11–17)

God gives us rules.

God keeps His promises.

God gives us courage.

We can trust God.

God answers prayers.

Memories

We all have people in our lives that teach us important things. Who taught you the following lessons?

(Fill in the blanks with names of people like Grandma, Grandpa, Mom, Dad, teacher, Sunday school teacher, pastor, sister, or brother. You can use more than one name on each line.)

Show kindness to others.

Have good manners.

Love God with all your heart.

Read God's Word.

Share with others.

Summertime

The skies of summer can be beautiful. The many colors of blue in the daytime, the brilliant colors of a sunset, and the sparkling diamonds in the night inspired David, the shepherd boy, to write the words in Psalm 19:1.

Use the following clues to fill in the blanks of David's psalm.

1. I am beyond the skies.
   The angels live in me.
   I am the _____ .

2. You can fly a kite in me.
   The birds love me.
   I am the _____ .

The (1.) — — — — declare the glory of God; the (2.) — — — — proclaim the work of His hands (Psalm 19:1).

I Will Glorify God

In each layer of ice cream, write or draw about a way to glorify God.

(Hints: worship, obey parents, share, etc.)

Fun Things of Summer

These pictures show things we see in summer. In each blank, write a word that describes how the pictures are similar.

THINGS tHat are in the _____.

THINGS tHat are _____.

THINGS tHat are at a _____.

THINGS tHat _____ GOD.

Nature Glorifies God

Everything in God's creation declares the glory of God. Think of things in nature that show the wonders of God's creation. Write them in blanks below.

The _____ declare the glory of God.

The _____ declare the glory of God.

The _____ declare the glory of God.

Draw a picture using some of the things you listed above.

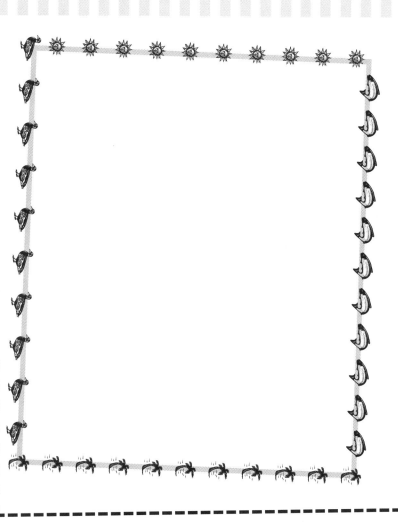

23

Show Kindness to Others

How are we to treat others? The words of Ephesians 4:32 will give you a clue.

Circle these words in the word search:

COMPASSIONATE ONE KIND AND

BE TO ANOTHER

```
V  R  S  Q  R  E  B  T
D  N  I  K  E  T  V  X
A  V  R  Q  H  A  Z  H
Z  W  U  Z  T  N  M  X
H  O  K  T  O  O  D  A
P  M  U  C  N  I  A  K
G  W  I  M  A  S  A  M
V  F  M  Y  Z  S  C  U
O  W  K  R  A  A  N  M
I  J  A  U  W  P  Q  E
R  N  N  T  K  M  N  U
D  A  O  K  X  O  I  I
N  R  X  W  T  C  O  D
```

Now use the words to write the Bible verse.

_____

_____ (Ephesians 4:32a).

I Will Show Kindness

Below is a list of things some children might do. Do they all show kindness? Write *yes* or *no* by each one.

At School

_____ Talk while the teacher is talking.

_____ Make fun of other children.

_____ Share your lunch treat with someone who needs a friend.

At Home

_____ Take cookies to a neighbor.

_____ Do an extra chore for your mom without being asked.

_____ Hit your brother for playing with your toys.

At Church

_____ Refuse to share your hymn book with your sister.

_____ Offer to help your Sunday school teacher put things away.

_____ Introduce yourself to a visitor.

Fill in the blank.

This week I will show kindness by _____.

Bible Kindness

Many people in the Bible showed kindness. Circle the examples that show love and kindness. Cross out the ones that do not.

King Darius threw Daniel into the lions' den.

David prayed for his enemies.

Jesus fed 5,000 people.

Jesus healed many sick people.

Men beat and crucified Jesus.

Dorcas sewed clothes for the poor.

Jesus died for our sins.

Showing Kindness

Circle each word that tells something about the picture.

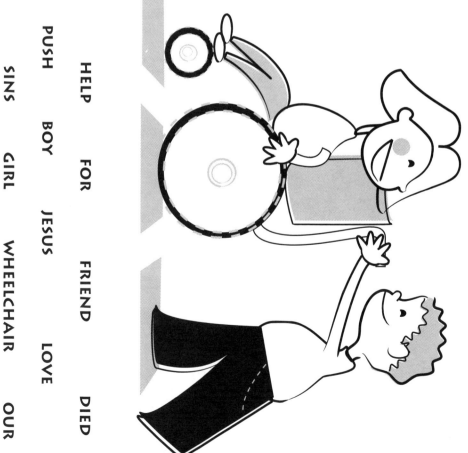

HELP   FOR   FRIEND   DIED

PUSH   BOY   JESUS   LOVE

SINS   GIRL   WHEELCHAIR   OUR

Use the leftover words to make a sentence about Jesus and His love for us.

_____ _____ _____ _____ _____ _____ .

Confessing Sins

"I'm sorry" are two of the hardest words to say. Fill in the blanks with the correct letters to learn what the Bible tells us about these words.

Key

a=◇ e=□ i=☆ o=♡ u=○

Th__ r __ f __ r __ c __ nf __ s s

y __ __ r s __ ns t __ __ ch

__ th __ r __ nd pr __ y

f __ r __ __ ch __ th __ r (James 5:16).

I Will Confess My Sins

Is there anyone you have sinned against? Ask God to help you say, "I'm sorry."

Sin I Will Confess

Person I've Hurt	Sin I Will Confess

Maybe these words will help:

DAD	MOM	SISTER
BROTHER	TEACHER	FRIEND
DISOBEYING	LYING	CHEATING	TEASING

But most of all, we can tell God that we are sorry. Ask God to help you confess your sins and forgive others.

© 2001 Carla Williams   Used by permission of Concordia Publishing House

An Important Word

Look at each clue. Find the letter that is different and write it in the blank. Then read the letters from top to bottom to find out what God helps you do when you have sinned.

This Letter is in:

____ cold but not old.

____ hold but not held.

____ nice but not ice.

____ feat but not eat.

____ peck but not pack.

____ strain but not train.

____ shop but not hop.

Words of Confession

David often confessed his sins. Look up the verses in your Bible and choose the correct word to write in each blank.

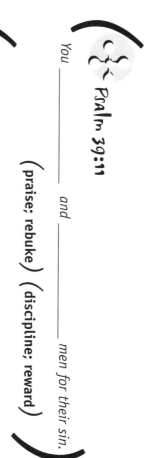

Psalm 32:5

Then I _____ my sin to you.

(**acknowledged, denied**)

Psalm 38:18

I _____ my iniquity; I am _____ by my sin.

(**hid; confessed**) (**troubled; comforted**)

Psalm 39:11

You _____ and _____ men for their sin.

(**praise; rebuke**) (**discipline; reward**)

Psalm 51:3

For I _____ my transgressions, and my sin is _____ before me.

(**know; like**) (**never; always**)

25

Being a Good Friend

Who is your best friend? What do you like to do with your friend? Do you and your friend ever disagree?

You have another friend who is the very best Friend of all. He always loves you. He gave the greatest gift of love. Follow the maze to this best Friend.

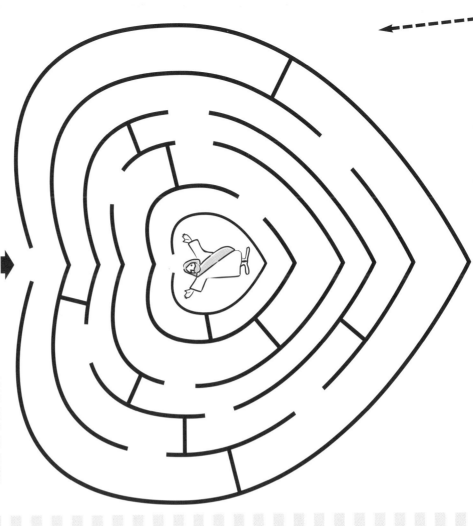

A friend loves at all times (Proverbs 17:17).

Tell a Friend

Look at the picture. Are they being a good friend?

Write some advice you could give about how to be a friend that shows God's love to others.

Friend for Life

Jonathan and David were best friends. They loved each other like brothers. Read 1 Samuel 18:1–4, 19:1–6, and 20:1–17 to learn about their special friendship.

Cross out all the X's and Y's in the box. Then fill in the blanks to find a message from the story.

```
J X O N A T H Y A N X Y X X X Y Y
X X X L O X X Y V E Y X D Y X X X
Y Y X X D X A X X Y V X I D Y X Y
A X Y Y X X X S X X X X Y X X X X
X H X Y I X M X S E X Y Y L X X F
```

_ _ _ _ _ _ _ _   _ _ _ _ _   _ _ _ _ _

_ _ _ _ _ _ _   _ _ _ _ _ _ _ .

Love your neighbor as yourself (Mark 12:31).

Jesus Is a Friend

The book of John tells about the many ways Jesus showed His love and kindness. Draw a line from each verse to what we can learn from Jesus.

Serve others   John 15:12

Pray for others   John 13:3–5

Love others   John 20:23

Forgive others   John 14:1

Trust each other   John 17:20

Can you think of any other traits of a good friend? Write them down.

_ _

_ _

A Special Day for Dad

Use the telephone pad to decode a message for you from Proverbs 1:8. This is a good message to remember on Father's Day.

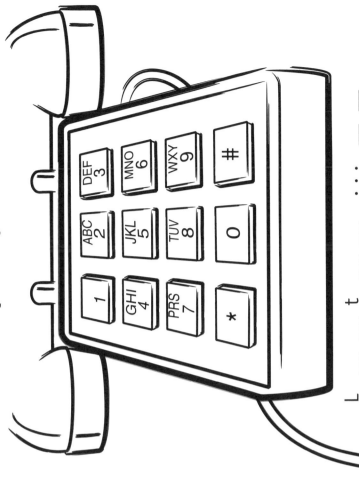

L t __ __ __ __ . . . __ __
5 __ 4 7 8 3 6 __ 8 6

y __ __ __
9 6 8 7

f __ __ __ __ '__ __
3 2 8 4 3 7 7

I __ s t __ __ __ __ __ __ __ __ .
4 6 7 8 7 8 2 8 4 6 6

Secret Message to Dad

Use the telephone pad on the front page to write a secret message to your dad or grandfather. Use words like love, thank you, kind, and obey. Have him try to figure out the message using the telephone pad.

A secret message for

God is your heavenly Father who gives you a dad to help lead, guide, and care for you. In the space below, write a poem or a message for your dad telling him what you like best about the things he does for you.

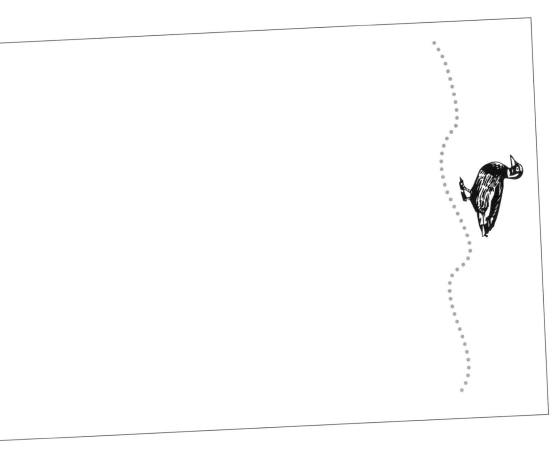

Picture This!

What is your favorite thing to do with Dad? In the frame below, draw a picture of you and Dad doing just that.

Say a prayer to God, thanking Him for the gift of your dad. Add any special requests on the lines provided.

Dear God,

_____

_____

_____

In Jesus' name, Amen.

sharing

In the Bible we read about a little boy who shared his lunch. Jesus performed a miracle and fed 5,000 people with the boy's small lunch.

Do the math problems to find out how many fishes and loaves of bread the boy shared. Draw the correct number of fish and loaves in the boy's basket.

2 + 10 - 3 + 1 - 5 = _____ (loaves)

4 + 3 - 1 + 3 - 7 = _____ (fish)

How many baskets were left over?

2 x 1 x 12 ÷ 2 = _____

[The believers] shared everything they had (Acts 4:32).

I will share with Others

One of the most important things to share is your faith in Jesus. Use the number key to fill in the blanks and find out with whom you can share Jesus.

Key

A	B	C	D	E	F	G	H	I	J	K	L	M	N	O	P	Q	R	S	T	U	V	W	X	Y	Z
3	8	26	17	4	32	9	43	59	1	7	12	56	83	14	2	30	55	6	11	5	10	20	60	74	96

___ ___ ___ ___ ___ ___
32 55 59 4 83 17 6

___ ___ ___ ___ ___ ___
83 4 59 9 43 8 14 55

___ ___ ___ ___ ___
11 4 3 26 43 4 55

___ ___ ___ ___
26 14 3 26 43

Can you name more?

Sharing Everything They Had

The people in the very first church shared everything they had. They did this because they loved Jesus and one another. What things can you share with others? Circle the items in each room that you could share.

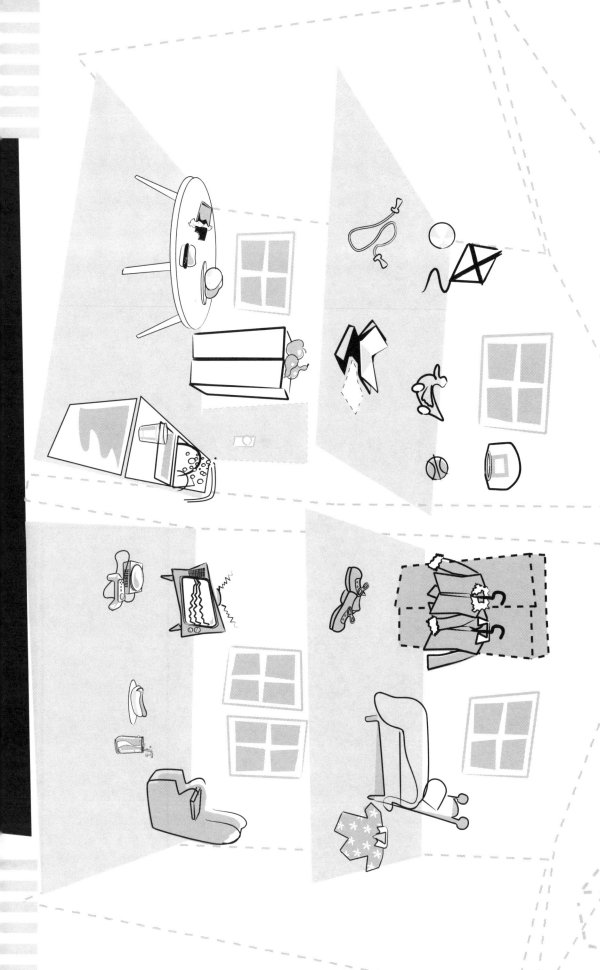

28

Freedom in Christ

Sin is like the strongest chain ever made. There is only one thing that can break the chain of sin.

Begin at the arrow and go counterclockwise. Write down every other letter in the chain to see what Jesus does for us.

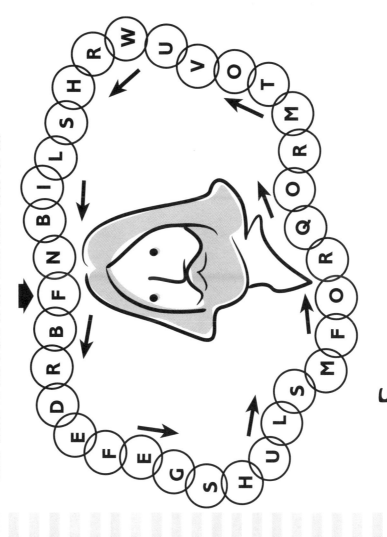

F _ _ _ _ _ _ _ _ _

If the Son sets you free, you will be free indeed (John 8:36).

Jesus Sets Me Free

Jesus died to free us from sin. Draw jail bars over the sins that you want Jesus to lock up in your life.

hatred   **patience**

cheating

lying   helpfulness

joy

making
fun of others

sharing   **hitting**

anger   *love*

selfishness

© 2001 Carla Williams   Used by permission of Concordia Publishing House

In Prison for God

Peter was put in jail because he told people about Jesus. Find out who freed Peter by completing the dot-to-dot below.

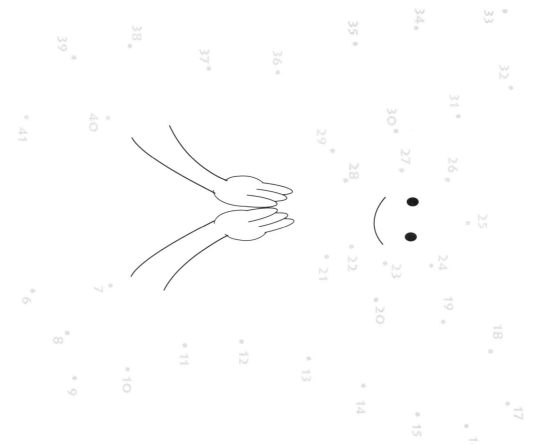

Free Indeed

Paul and Silas were put in prison for preaching about Jesus. Even though they were in chains, they sang praises to the Lord. God used an earthquake to break their chains and set them free. The jailer took Paul and Silas to his home. He and his family became followers of Christ.

Count the letters in the jailhouse. Which letter did you count 8 times? 4 times? 10 times? Write the correct letter on each blank at the bottom of the page.

The jailer was set free from his _____ _____ .

8 times   4 times   10 times

The Good Shepherd

There are many different ways to picture Jesus. Read each clue, then find the letters that spell out the same thing.

King or Master (4-letter word)   A L H O T R I D M

Belonging to me (2-letter word)   T J M K I Y O

Sheep herder (7-letter word)   S K J H E Q P J H E S R D

Rhymes with "got" (3-letter word)   M K N U H O L T

Wish for something (4-letter word)   W K L A R N G T

Use the words you found to complete the Bible verse.

The __ __ __ is __ __ __ __ __ __ __, I shall __ __ __ be in __ __ __ __ (Psalm 23:1).

Following the Good Shepherd

Read John 10:1–16 to find out how Jesus is our Good Shepherd. Draw a line between each verse and the phrase that shows how Jesus shepherds us.

Know His voice

The gate to God

Lays down His life

Protects us

John 10:7

John 10:11

John 10:12

John 10:16

Psalm 23

Psalm 23 tells us that the Lord cares for us like a shepherd cares for his sheep. Use words from Psalm 23 to find the answers to this puzzle.

Across

2. God gives us so much that our heart ____.

4. The opposite of bad or evil.

6. God takes care of us so even our ____ can see He loves us.

8. He restores my ____.

10. I will not be afraid of ____ ...

12. ... because I will live with God ____.

Down

1. God leads me down paths of ____.

3. The Lord is my ____.

5. His ____ guides and comforts me.

7. God leads me to ____ places.

9. I will not fear the devil or any ____.

11. God makes me rest in green ____.

Rejoice Always

Cross out all letters that appear four times. Arrange the letters that are left over to complete the message from the Bible you can use in both good and bad times.

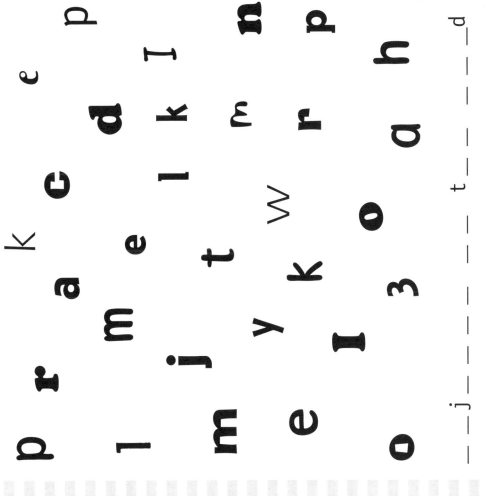

p   k   m

p   a   c   d   e   p

r   k

l   m   e   l   k   I

m   j   t   m   n

y   k   w   r   p

e   l   o   q   h

o   3

j _ _ _ _ _ _ _ t _ _ _ d

a _ _ _ _ _ _

(Philippians 4:4)

I Will Rejoice Always

Do you rejoice at these times? Circle your answer.

Ask Jesus to help you rejoice, no matter what!

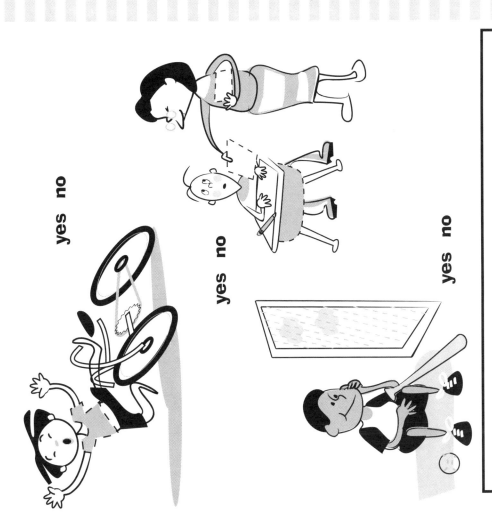

yes no

yes no

yes no

The apostle Paul tells us to rejoice always, even when things are difficult. Solve the rebus words below to find out what kinds of things Paul rejoiced in.

1.

 - e +  - c + ings

_____ _____ _____ _____ _____ _____

2.

 + less  - k = s

_____ _____ _____ _____ _____

3.

 - t + rd + - l

_____ _____ _____ _____ _____ !

Always Joyful

Look up these Bible verses and fill in the blanks to learn more about the times Paul rejoiced. You might be surprised!

✳ **(Acts 16:22)**

The crowd joined in the _____ against Paul and Silas, and the magistrates ordered them to be _____ and _____.

✳ **(Acts 23:2)**

At this the high priest Ananias ordered those standing near Paul to _____ him on the _____.

✳ **(2 Corinthians 12:10)**

That is why, for Christ's sake, I delight in weaknesses, in _____, in _____, in persecutions, in _____.

For when I am weak, then I am strong.

✳ **(2 Corinthians 11:27)**

I have labored and _____ and have often gone without _____; I have known _____ and thirst and have often gone without _____; I have been cold and _____.

Forgiveness

FORGIVE is hidden seven times in the puzzle. Circle the word FORGIVE each time you find it.

Y	M	F	O	R	G	I	V	E	T	U	E
F	O	R	G	I	V	E	B	V	S	V	C
O	W	P	D	E	M	C	X	I	I	Y	Q
R	T	R	S	P	F	O	R	G	I	V	E
G	L	N	B	E	T	D	R	R	U	K	J
I	Q	A	Z	X	S	O	W	O	T	H	G
V	F	V	N	E	F	K	W	F	P	L	M
E	V	I	G	R	O	F	Q	I	E	X	L

Forgive as the Lord forgave you (Colossians 3:13).

Forgive As Jesus Forgave

In each box trace the arrow from Jesus to the word ME if Christ has forgiven you for doing this sin. Then trace the arrow from ME to the children if you need to forgive someone else for doing this to you.

me

me

Making fun of someone.

me

me

Breaking something that belongs to someone else.

me

me

Hurting someone else.

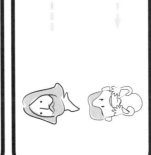

7o Times

The disciples wanted to know how many times they should forgive. The number Jesus told them was HUGE—showing that we are to forgive others A LOT!

Do the math below to see which answer matches the number in Matthew 18:22. Circle the answer that matches.

200 + 250 + 40 = _____

12 x 5 = _____

49 ÷ 7 = _____

90 - 53 + 8 = _____

11 x 7 = _____

(2 x 3) + 1 = _____

15 + 30 + 24 - 2 + 10 = _____

How many times will YOU forgive?

The Meaning of Forgiveness

Look up the Bible verses to find a word that begins with each of the letters in F-O-R-G-I-V-E. Each word relates to forgiveness.

F _____ **(John 8:36)**

O _____ **(Revelation 3:21)**

R _____ **(Luke 6:35)**

G _____ **(Psalm 69:16)**

I _____ * **(Psalm 25:11)**

V _____ **(1 Corinthians 15:56–57)**

E _____ **(Proverbs 25:21)**

*This word means the same as sins.

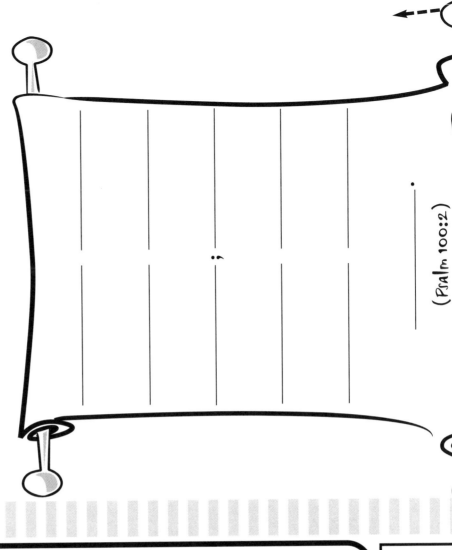

32

Worshiping God

Psalm 100 is used for giving thanks. In worship we give thanks for the many blessings God gives us. Look up Psalm 100:2 to discover how we are to worship God, our Maker. Write the verse on the scroll below.

_____

_____

_____

_____ ;

_____

_____

_____

_____ .

(Psalm 100:2)

How I Will Worship God?

Solve each row of math problems. Then match the answers to the key and write the correct letters in each blank.

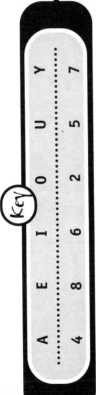

key	A	E	I	O	U	Y
	4	8	6	2	5	7

R ___ J ___ ___ ___ C ___
4 + 4 ___ 6 - 4 ___ 5 + 1 ___ 12 - 4 ___

___ L ___ W ___ ___ S ___
10 - 6 ___ 2 x 2 ___ 5 + 2 ___

AND

P R ___ ___
4 x 1 ___ 3 + 4 ___

___ C ___ N ___ T ___ N ___ ___ L L ___ .
10 - 8 ___ 3 x 2 ___ 8 - 3 ___ 7 - 3 ___ 5 + 2 ___

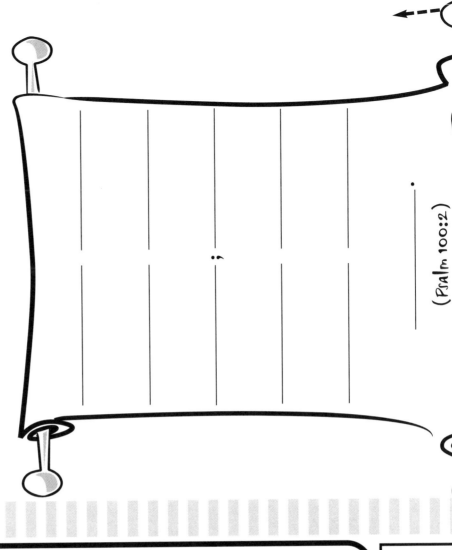

© 2001 Carla Williams   Used by permission of Concordia Publishing House

The Israelites Worship God

God's people, the Israelites, were slaves in Egypt. The Egyptians worshiped many idols and gods. Pharaoh made the Israelites build great structures that represented the kings and gods of Egypt. The Israelites wanted to leave Egypt so they could worship the one true God.

Circle the hidden pictures: 7 Israelites praying, 1 set of stone tablets, 2 tambourines, and 2 horns.

33

Cheerfulness

Put the words in the proper order to find out what is "good medicine" for a follower of Jesus.

GOOD

IS

HEART

A

CHEERFUL

MEDICINE

(Proverbs 17:22)

Having a Cheerful Heart

Write what you can do to bring joy to those named in each heart.

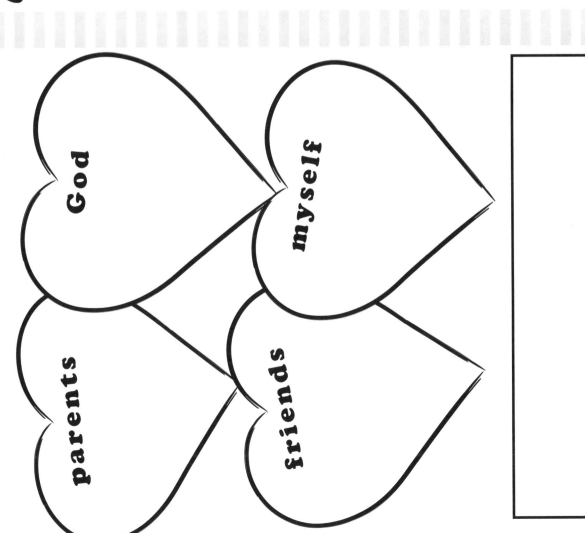

God

parents

myself

friends

Dance for Joy

Look up Exodus 15:19–21 to discover what Miriam did when God saved the Israelites from Pharaoh's army.

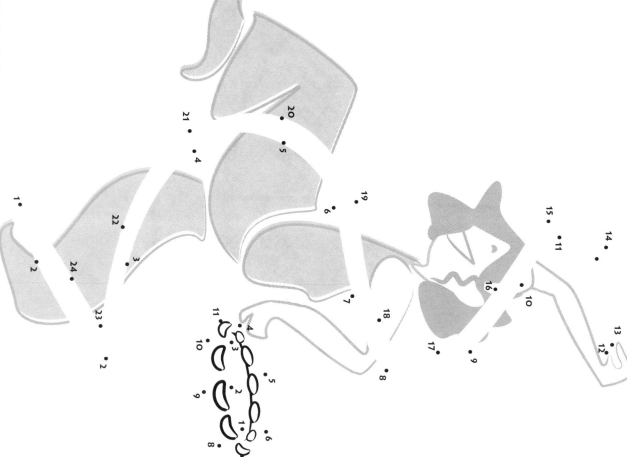

Cheerful Riddles

Identify these people from the Bible who showed their joy.

_ _ _ _ _ _

(She opened the door to find a wonderful surprise.)

_ _ _

(He turned somersaults in his mother's womb.)

_ _ _ _ of _ _ _ _

(God accepted their offering and they shouted for joy.)

_ _ _ _ _

(10 - 9 means only one rejoiced.)

_ _ _ _ _

(He jumped from a boat to see his friend.)

If you need help, look up these verses from Scripture: Luke 1:41, Acts 12:13–14, Leviticus 9:23–24, Luke 17:12–19, John 21:7.

Starting a new school year can be a little scary. But there is someone who goes with you—whether or not you are scared. Help this student find out who is with her as she goes to school.

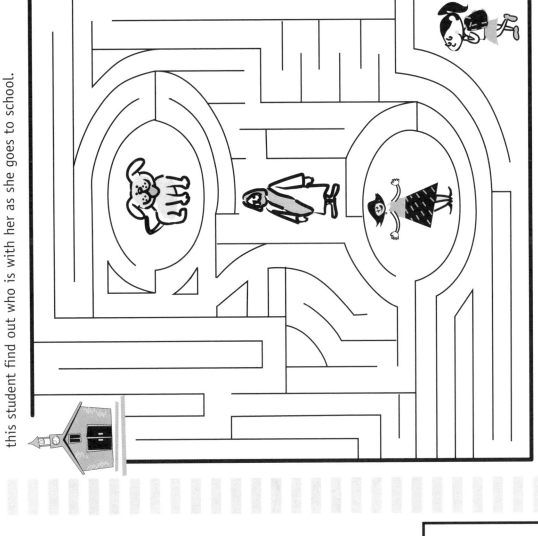

I am with you always (Matthew 28:20).

Jesus Is with Me

How can you take Jesus to school with you?

Fill in the blanks with your choices.

I can _____ before going to school.

I can carry a small Bible in my _____.

I will tell others about _____.

Look carefully at this picture. Can you tell which children know that Jesus is with them?

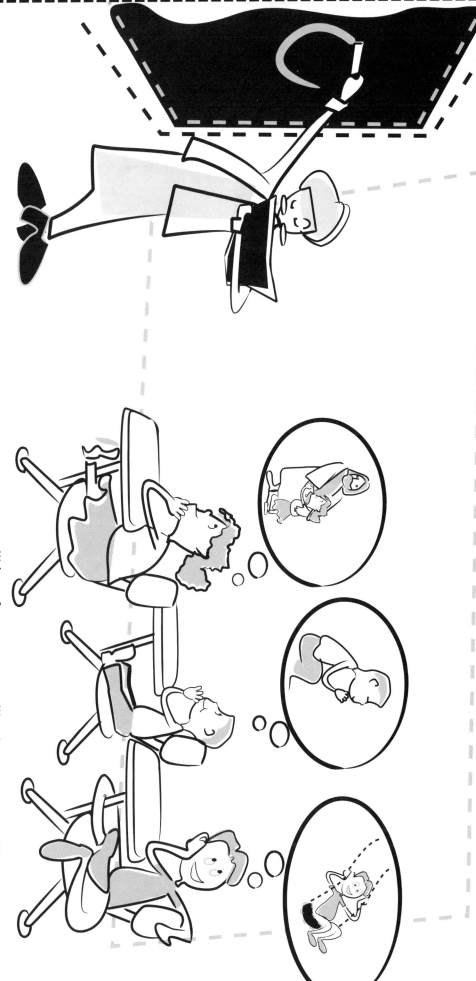

Write a few sentences telling how Jesus is in YOUR classroom.

35

Rest in the Lord

What does the word *rest* mean? Usually it means to lie down or to stop doing an activity for awhile.

In Psalm 62:5 the word *rest* has a different meaning. Choose the correct words to complete the Bible verse. Did you learn a new meaning for the word *rest*?

_____ , O my soul,
(Lose, Find)

_____ alone; my
(work, rest)

in _____
(myself, God)

_____ from _____
(hope, fear)   (Him, her)

_____ (Psalm 62:5).
(goes, comes)

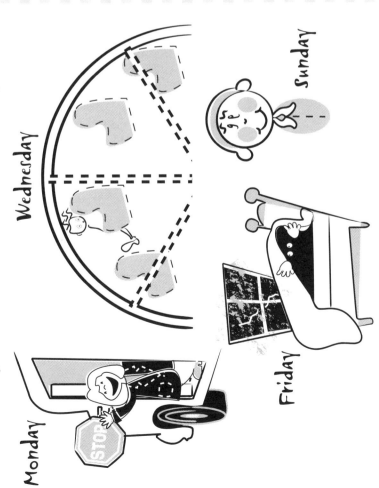

I Rest in God

Write how you will rest in the Lord on each of these days.

Monday

Wednesday

Friday

Sunday

Monday _____

Wednesday _____

Friday _____

Sunday

Rest in God—No Matter What

When we "rest" in the Lord, we give all our worries and cares to Him. Look up the Bible verses below and draw a line from the names of the people to the situation when they rested in the Lord.

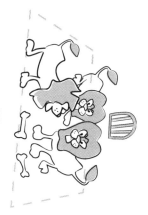

Joseph (Genesis 39:20–23)

Daniel (Daniel 6:16–23)

Disciples (Luke 8:23–25)

Shadrach, Meshach, and Abednego
(Daniel 3:16–28)

Hard Workers

Think about some of the people you know in your church. Put a ✔ by the jobs you know some of them have.

___ doctor

___ waitress

___ homemaker

___ nurse

___ computer technician

___ teacher

___ construction worker

___ police officer

___ engineer

___ store clerk

___ babysitter

___ firefighter

___ pilot

What do you think you might like to do when you grow up?

_____

36

Loving God's Word

Words in the Bible sometimes paint pictures to help us understand what God is teaching. Put the words in order and connect the dots to discover what God's Word is in our lives.

your *lamp* *a* *path* *Word* *my* *is* *to* *light* *to* *and* *feet* *a* *my*

_____
_____
_____

(Psalm 119:105).

God's Word Lights My Way

God's Word lights our path like a flashlight in the dark. Read through the word list. Circle the words that show God is shining through you.

Word list:

BITTERNESS

ANGER

JOY

SYMPATHY

LOVE

SELF-CONTROL

PEACE

JEALOUSY

HATRED

SELFISHNESS

Look up each Bible verse. Match the pictures of the men who loved God with their stories.

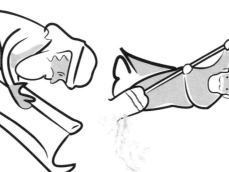
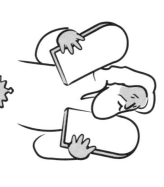

Ezra 7:10

Exodus 33:12–13

Luke 4:16–17

2 Chronicles 34:8

Special Verses about God's Word

Draw a picture showing what each Bible verse means to you.

Hear the Word of the Lord (Jeremiah 21:11).

I will not neglect Your Word (Psalm 119:16).

In the beginning was the Word (John 1:1).

37

Tell Others about Jesus

There is a difference between just *knowing about* Jesus and really *following* Him. A disciple is one who truly believes and follows Jesus.

Circle the children below who are showing they are followers of Jesus. Put an ✖ on the children who are not.

Therefore go and make disciples of all nations (Matthew 28:19).

Who Can I Tell about Jesus?

Complete this crossword puzzle to discover where you can tell people about Jesus.

Across

2. A place where you buy food (2 words).
4. An outdoor place to play.
6. Where children like to shop.

Down

2. Stop here when your car runs low on gas (2 words).
3. Children go here to learn.
5. You will find many video games here.

Jesus said to make disciples in all nations. Look at the pictures below. Match the style of native costume with the correct country around the world.

China

Holland

Africa

Mexico

Fishing for People

Jesus explained that making disciples is like fishing for people. Use the code below to identify the names of different countries.

KEY

| a | e | i | o | u |

N — g — r — — —

C h — n —

B r — z — l

F r — n c —

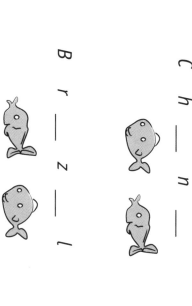

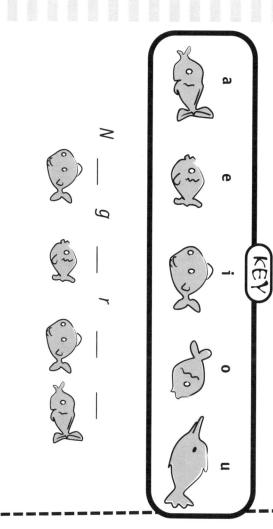

The Body of Christ

All believers are part of the body of Christ and each one has important work to do. Draw a chain of hearts to connect the people below. Remember that God is helping each of them to serve.

So in Christ we who are many form one body,
and each member belongs to all the others (Romans 12:5).

The Body Works Together

Solve the puzzle to discover two ways the body of Christ works together.

1. __ __ __ __ __ __ __ __ __
E3 A1 D4 D2   B5 B1   B5 A2 D2

__ __ __ .
A3 B1 D3

2. __ __ __ __ __ __ __ __ __ __ __ __ __ __ __ __ __ __
E1 E2 A3 A3 B1 D3 B5   D6 A1 E1 E1 A1 B1 A5 B2 D3 A1 D2 E1

Key

Follow the grid below to find each mystery letter above.
(Example: the letter for C3 is M).

	1	2	3	4	5	6
A	I	h	p	d	n	w
B	o	a	c	q	t	y
C	b	k	m	j	f	z
D	l	e	r	v	a	m
E	s	u	g	z	x	p

© 2001 Carla Williams   Used by permission of Concordia Publishing House

Everyone Is Important

Each part of our body has its own job.
Look up the following verses and write them in the blanks next
to the corresponding body parts.

1 Thessalonians 4:11   Psalm 121:1   Ephesians 6:14

John 13:5   Colossians 3:15   Romans 15:6

One Body

Read the following rebus to learn about the body of Christ.

The  says that each  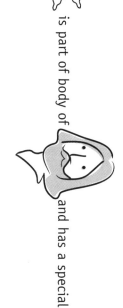 is a special

part of the [church] . Just like your [foot] and [hand]

R an important part of your [body] , so each [fish/body]

is part of body of [body of Christ] and has a special

job to do. No [cup] [sun] [cup] [sun] is more important than another.

38

39

God Cares for Me

We have many needs like food, water, clothing, friendship, and shelter. To find out why God provides for us, change each letter to the one that comes *after* it in the alphabet.

B _ G _ Q _ H _ R _ S _

I _ D _ R _ T _ R _

Write the letters you found above onto the blanks below.

My God will meet all your needs ... in

_ _ _ _ _ _ _ _ _ _ _ _ _

(Philippians 4:19)

His Banner over Me

The Bible tells us that God holds a banner of love over us at all times. Design a banner showing that God loves and cares for you.

God took care of the Israelites while they were in the desert. Read each Bible verse and draw a line to the things that God provided His people.

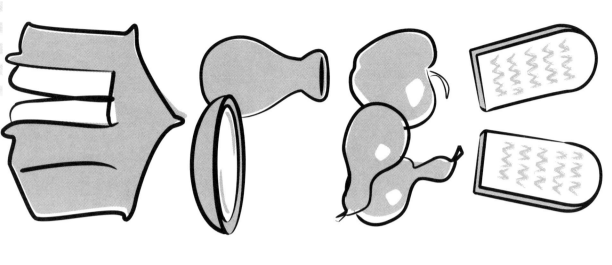

Exodus 16:31

Exodus 17:6

Exodus 25:8–9

Deuteronomy 5:31

The Good Samaritan

The parable of the Good Samaritan helps us understand how God sometimes uses people to care for our needs.

What needs did the Good Samaritan provide for in order to take care of the hurt man? Find the jug of water, bandages, food, money, and the inn.

Autumn

Unscramble the words on each leaf. Write each new word onto a blank.

dsefil

oyj

sterof

lbjntaiu

igns

stere

_____

_____

_____

Place the words from the blanks above onto the blanks below.

Let the _____ be _____, and everything in them.

Then all the _____ of the _____ will _____

for _____ (Psalm 96:12).

Thank You for Harvest Time

In the harvest of the fields, God provides us with food. Circle these foods in the word search.

CORN   BREAD   SQUASH   WHEAT   APPLES   PUMPKIN

CRANBERRIES   TURKEY

```
G  O  D  P  R  O  T  V  Y  H  S  I
D  E  S  G  O  A  O  E  S  E  E  D
T  N  H  I  E  N  K  A  I  G  L  S
Z  I  R  H  R  U  R  S  I  P  X
B  K  W  L  U  Q  R  G  W  F  P  Z
X  P  J  T  S  E  C  D  N  V  A  H
T  M  A  T  B  O  R  O  A  A  N  F
O  U  O  N  R  Z  B  P  V  E  F  M
H  P  A  N  D  D  G  O  Y  G  R  M
K  R  E  Q  L  E  S  G  Y  A  M  B
C  J  O  I  F  M  O  T  A  D  R  J
U  K  J  Y  E  G  K  S  N  G  I  G
```

Starting with the G, write the letters that are left over into the blanks below until you spell out a hidden message.

_ _ _ _ _ _ _ _ _ _ _ _ .

© 2001 Carla Williams   Used by permission of Concordia Publishing House

Harvest Time

The weather cools, and the leaves change from green to orange, yellow, and red. The crops ripen in the fields and are harvested. Autumn reminds us that God provides for us.

Find these signs of autumn in the picture:

rake   hoe   loaf of bread   pumpkin   cornucopia

scarecrow   ear of corn

Add your own signs of autumn to the picture.

41

Obedience

Put the tiles together to make the words that belong in the Bible verse. Cross out each tile as you use it. The first one has been done for you.

LO

REN

IS

YO

IS

TH

PA

~~CHI~~

EY

FOR

REN

HT

RIG

UR

OB

IN

LD

TS

THE

RD

CHI _____ , _____ _____ _____ _____

_____ (EPHESIANS 6:1).

I Will Obey

Think of ways you can obey your parents. Use each letter in the word *obedience*. One sample has been done for you.

O _____

B _____

E *at whatever Mom makes for dinner.*

D _____

I _____

E _____

N _____

C _____

E _____

Obedient Children

There are many examples of children in the Bible who obeyed their parents. In fact, Luke 2:51 tells us that Jesus obeyed His earthly parents.

Unscramble the names of these Bible parents and children.

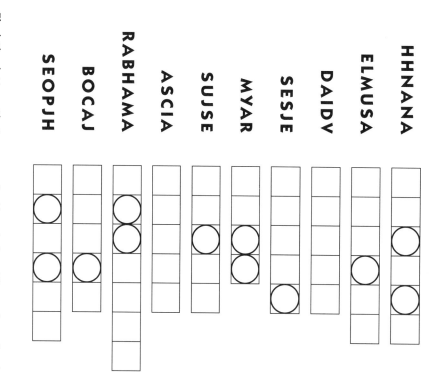

HHNANA

ELMUSA

DAIDV

SESJE

MYAR

SUSE

ASCIA

RABHAMA

BOCAJ

SEOPJH

Find the letters that appear in the circles. Place them in the blanks below for the final message.

— — — — — — — — Y — — — — P — — — T — .

Others Who Obeyed

Look up the Bible verses below to find out who obeyed whom.

1 Chronicles 21:19

——— obeyed .

Acts 5:29

——— and the ——— obeyed ——— .

Genesis 28:7

——— obeyed his ——— and ——— .

Numbers 15:37–41

——— obeyed ——— .

Grumbling

Do everything without complaining or arguing, so that you may ... shine like stars in the universe (Philippians 2:14).

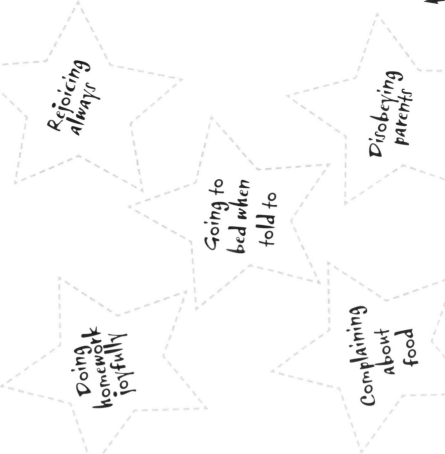

Rejoicing always

Going to bed when told to

Disobeying parents

Doing homework joyfully

Complaining about food

Read the words in each star and decide which ones shine God's love in the universe. Trace around these stars to make them shine.

Jesus Helps Me Not to Grumble

What chores or homework do you dislike most? Write a prayer inside the heart asking Jesus to help you do these tasks with gladness instead of grumbling.

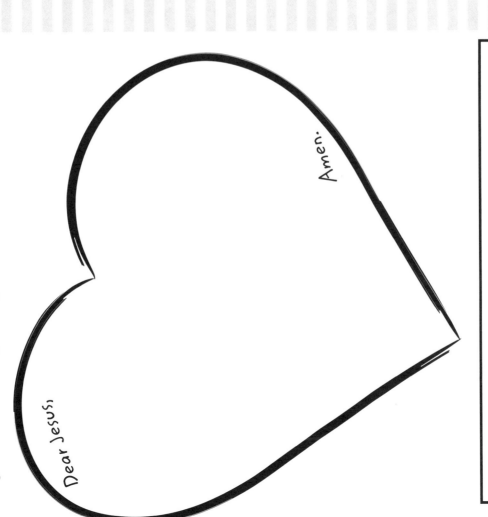

Dear Jesus,

Amen.

© 2001 Carla Williams   Used by permission of Concordia Publishing House

Words Say a Lot

Words we use tell others how we feel. Think about how God wants you to talk to other people.

Put a ♡ around words that show you are content and rejoicing. Put an ✘ on words that show grumbling and complaining.

Yuck!

Please

NO WAY!

Stupid

Love

Thank you

Good

Hate

Shining in My Family

The Bible verse teaches that we shine God's love to others when we do things without complaining or grumbling. Look at the picture below. Which words tell you something about the picture?

ENJOYING   FIGHTING   FUN   GRUMBLING

COOPERATION   WASHING   ARGUING

Make a list of other words that describe the family in the picture.

_____

_____

_____

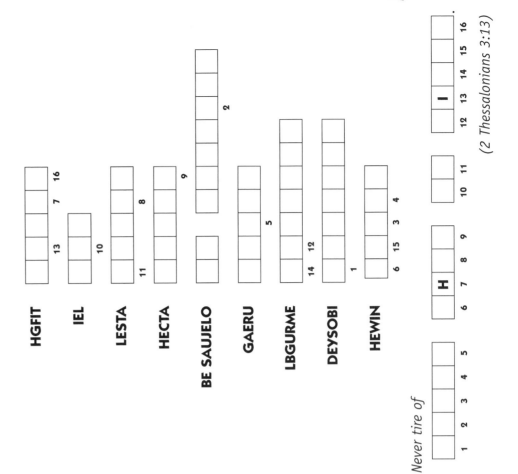

43

Doing What Is Right

We all sin and do things that are wrong. But Jesus forgives our sins and He helps us make the right choices to do what is right.

Unscramble the clue words. Then copy the letters in the numbered squares into the squares with the same number in the Bible verse below.

HGFIT

□□□□ □
13 7 16

IEL

□□
10

LESTA

□□□□□
11   8

HECTA

□□□□□
9

BE SAUJELO

□□□□□□□□□
2

GAERU

□□□□□
14 12   5

LBGURME

□□□□□□□
1

DEYSOBI

□□□□□□□
6 15 3 4

HEWIN

□□□□□
6 7 8 9

Never tire of

□□□□□
1 2 3 4 5

□ **H** □
6

□□□ □□
7 8 9 10 11

□ **I** □
12 13 14 15 16

(2 Thessalonians 3:13)

The Right Sign

Doing what is right and pleasing to God is a way of saying "I LOVE YOU" to God.

Finish the dot-to-dot below to discover how to say "I LOVE YOU" in sign language.

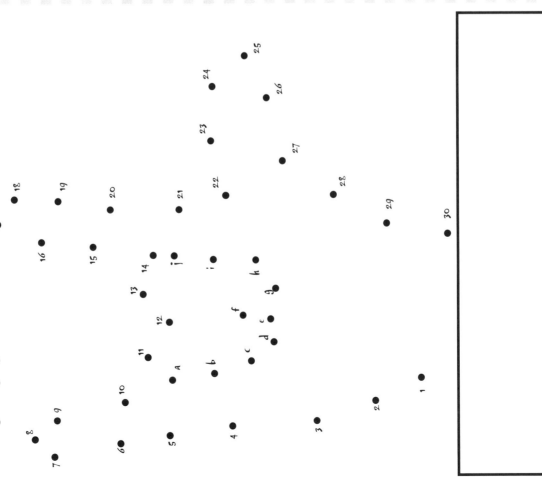

Doing Right for Jesus

Doing the right thing is one way to show the love of Jesus to others. Under each picture write what the child is doing to share the love of Jesus.

This child is

.

This child is

.

We can tell others how much Jesus loves us. Write what you think this child might be saying.

This child is saying, "

."

Finding Help to Do What Is Right

Who can help you do what is right? Draw a line between the children that are exactly alike. Where the lines cross you will find the answer.

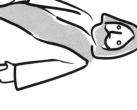

Honesty

Find these hidden words that relate to honesty.

CHEAT   FALSEHOODS   HONEST   HONESTY

HONORABLE   LIE   RIGHTEOUS   TRUTHFULLY

```
D O N O T L I E T O E A C H O
H T H E R D J T X C N J V G O
C O I S K E R E K O A G O V L
T O N G C W I C P L Y Q S S K
W A L O W L E W T G O L W I Z
E G E N R L S G H E Y Q G J F
P S E H F A R I G H T E O U S
X X L M C U B T A F U M K W Q
A A W A J N K L S I N Z R H T
Y X M X F W C K E E Y O T W N
T R U T H F U L L Y N U K U M
Y T S E N O H F B A R O R G I
F A L S E H O O D S Z N H R M
```

Write the leftover letters in order onto the blanks below until you spell out the Bible verse.

_____

(Colossians 3:9a)

Jesus, Help Me to Be Honest

Sometimes it's hard to be honest, but Jesus can help. Draw a line from Jesus to the pictures to show that He can help you tell the truth.

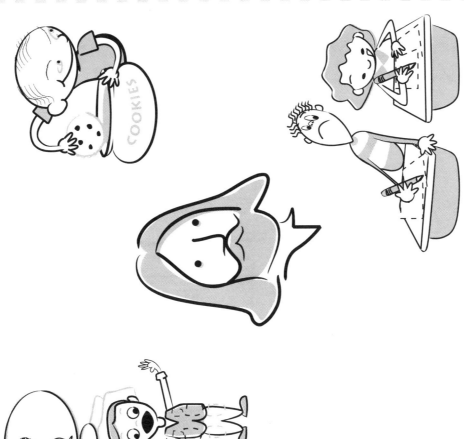

King Solomon Reveals a Lie

Two women came to King Solomon for help. They both had a baby boy, but one of the babies died. His mother switched babies. Then she lied and said that the alive baby was hers. But the other mother knew better. They went to King Solomon for help.

God had given King Solomon the gift of wisdom. He said to cut the alive baby in half and split him between the two women. The real mother cried and said, "Give the baby to her. Please do not kill him." Then King Solomon knew who the real mother was—the one who wanted to save the baby. He knew that the first woman had lied.

Which of these women is the real mother? Use the clues to figure out the answer.

Clues

The real mother is wearing a head scarf.
The real mother is crying.

Little Lies

You might think that using a little lie to cover up something you have done is okay. But even a little lie can turn into a big one.

These pictures tell the story of a little lie that turned into a big one. Put them in the correct order by placing 1, 2, 3, or 4 in each circle.

What was the boy's first lie?

How did the lie grow?

What should he have done instead?

45

Trust in the Lord

What do you do when you have troubles or fears? Look to this Bible verse to discover the best thing to do. Use the code to find out what it is.

_____ _____ _____ _____ _____ _____ _____ _____ _____ _____ _____

_____ _____ _____ _____ _____ _____ _____ _____

_____ _____ _____ _____ _____ _____ (_____ _____ _____ _____ 3:5).

Code

A - ✂   H - 🗝   O - ✷   T - ✝   Y - ✴

B - ✠   I - ✿   P - ✉   U - ✚

D - ✂   L - ☎   R - ☝   V - •

E - ✂   N - ☞   S - 9   W - ①

I Will Trust God

Here is a list of some things that might make you feel afraid.

You have a big test at school. _____

You are in a loud thunderstorm. _____

A dog in your neighborhood threatens you. _____

You need to cross a busy street. _____

You feel really sick. _____

Your family is moving to a new town. _____

Below is a list of ways you can place your trust in God. Select a letter or letters from this list and put one or more letters in the space next to the sentences above.

A. Tell God you are afraid.

B. Ask God to help you.

C. Ask someone else to pray with you.

D. Remember Proverbs 3:5.

People Who Trusted God

Read the sentences in the box. Then look at each picture and decide how each person trusted in God. Write the number that goes with each picture in the blank. (Look up their stories in the Bible for clues.)

1. Prayed to God
2. Had faith in God
3. Sang praise to God
4. Worshiped only God

David (1 Samuel 17:31-37) ____

Daniel (Daniel 6:10-23) ____

Shadrach, Meshach, and Abednego (Daniel 3:16-28) ____

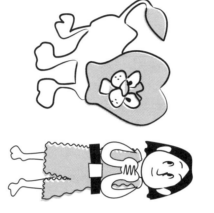

Paul & Silas (Acts 16:23-28) ____

Put Your Trust in God

Sometimes we put our trust in other things instead of in God. Unscramble the words to find out what these other things might be.

Then look up the Bible verses and draw a line matching each verse to an unscrambled word.

I W S M D O ____   Matthew 6:24

D O I L S ____   Jeremiah 9:23

E M Y O N ____   1 Corinthians 1:25

H T T R E G N S ____   Psalm 31:6

45

Better to Give than Receive

It feels great to get something from someone else. But the Bible tells us that it is even better to give than to receive.

Write the word **giving** or **receiving** on each blank.

The girl is _____ flowers to her mother.

The boy is _____ a present from his father.

The girl is _____ the sick man a pot of soup.

I Can Give to Others

Make a list of the blessings that you receive at home.

love

_____

_____

_____

_____

Now think of ways you can give to others at home.

speak kind words

_____

_____

_____

© 2001 Carla Williams   Used by permission of Concordia Publishing House

In the Bible we read about many people who shared with others. Look up these Bible verses and match the people with what they shared.

Dorcas (Acts 9:39)

Small Boy (John 6:5-12)

Believers in the
Early Church (Acts 4:32)

Lydia (Acts 16:13-15)

Things We Can Give Others

Draw a line from each word on the left to a word on the right that has only one different letter.

Draw a circle around the things in each column that you can give to someone else.

shirt	gift
love	good
cat	money
lunch	skirt
bug	dove
food	hug
honey	bunch
lift	bat

Give Thanks

Thanksgiving Day is not the only day we can give thanks. When do you give thanks to God for all of the wonderful things He has given you?

The missing words in the Bible verse will help you know when to give thanks.

Write the first letter of each picture on the blank next to it.

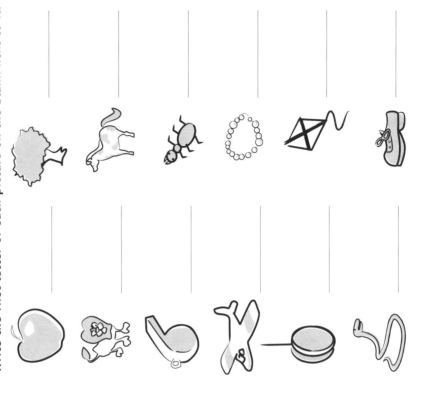

Now write the two new words you spelled above onto the blanks below.

_____ _____ to God the Father for everything, _____ giving _____ in the name of our Lord Jesus Christ (Ephesians 5:20).

Thank You, God

The Bible encourages us to give thanks at all times—even when it might seem hard. Write a simple prayer of thanksgiving for each picture.

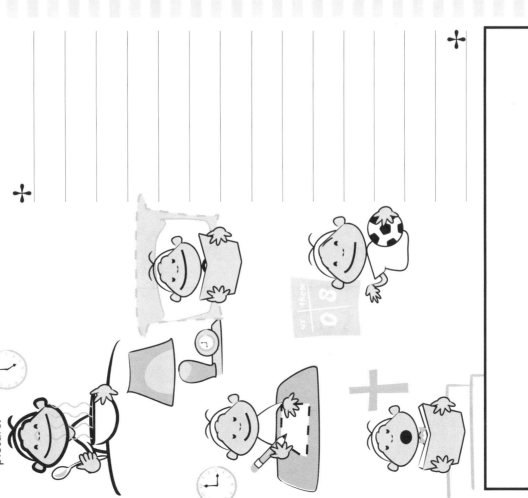

Words of Thanks

The Bible is full of passages about giving thanks. Look up the Bible verses below and draw a ♡ around the ones that tell about thanksgiving.

PSALM 28:7

Psalm 7:17

Philippians 4:6

Psalm 95:2

Psalm 136:1

Psalm 30:2

Galatians 5:22

Write out the verse you would most like to remember.

_____

_____

_____

_____

Wintertime

In some parts of the country, winter is marked by icy weather, windy days, and snow. What is winter like where you live?

Unscramble the order of the words on the snowmen and write them in the spaces below.

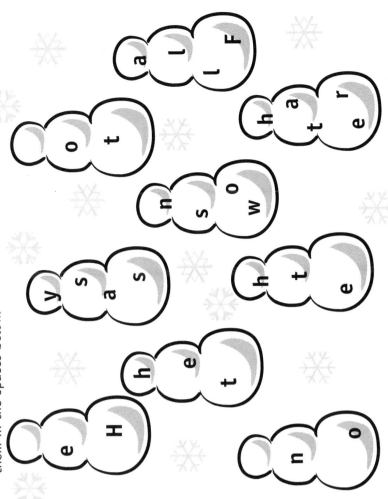

Winter Fun

Whenever it snows we can think of God who made the snow. If it does not snow where you live, the cool days of winter can give you extra time to read and study the Bible, to pray, and to reflect on God's goodness throughout the year.

Draw a picture of your favorite thing about winter where you live. Then finish the sentence below the picture.

Thank you God for _____.

"_____ _____, _____
(God)

_____" (Job 37:6).

Stop and Think about God

Here are the rest of the words to the Bible verse about snow:

"[God] says to the snow, 'Fall on the earth ... *so that all men He has made may know His work, He stops every man from his labor*'" (Job 37:6-7).

Job suggests that we should stop our work when it snows and think about the wonders of God. Write the word **stop** in the signs if that person should stop what they are doing when it starts to snow.

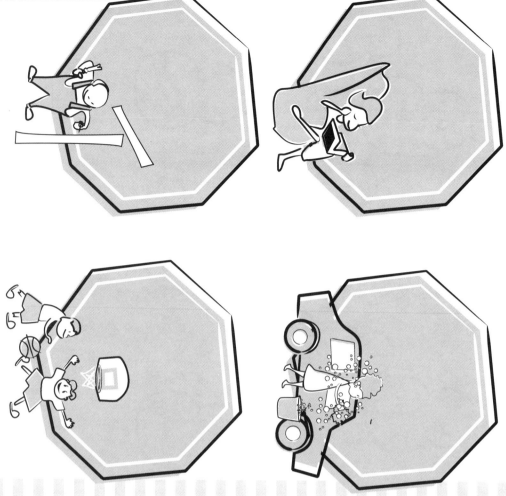

Snow Scriptures

Look up these verses about snow. See how these word pictures help us better understand God's words for us.

Write one word by each snowflake representing one of the verses. (Your words might include forgiveness, creation, refreshing, purity, and cleansing.)

Then draw a line from each word to the Bible verse it matches.

Psalm 51:7

Isaiah 1:18

Psalm 147:16

Isaiah 55:10

Matthew 28:3

48

Children of the Bible

In the Bible we read about children who loved God. See if you know their stories. Circle the name of the child that is shown in each picture.

David

Joseph

Timothy

Esther

Rebekah

Miriam

Daniel

Moses

Samuel

Moses

Joseph

David

Before I formed you in the womb I knew you, before you were born I set you apart (Jeremiah 1:5).

God Has Called Me

God calls each of us to do His work. Some people become pastors, or missionaries, or teachers. No matter what you grow up to do, God calls you to do your work for Him.

Fill in the blanks below. Look over your answers and see if you can think of something that God may be calling you to do.

My favorite hobbies are _____.

When I grow up I think I would like to _____.

My best subject in school is _____.

My favorite person in the Bible is _____.

My favorite Bible verse is _____.

Say this prayer:

Dear God, Thank You for making me Your child. I trust that You have special plans for me that will bring glory to You. In Jesus' name I pray. Amen.

© 2001 Carla Williams   Used by permission of Concordia Publishing House

God's Plan in Our Life

Each of these children were part of God's special plan. He had a special purpose for each one of them. Draw a line between the child and the job God chose for each one as they grew up. Look up the Bible verses if you need clues.

Joseph
Genesis 45:7–8

Moses
Exodus 3:10

David
1 Samuel 16:11–13

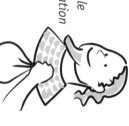

Esther
Esther 4:12–14

Saves her people
from death

King of Israel

Lead people
out of Egypt

Saves people
from starvation

Lessons by Example

We can learn from the children in the Bible and the special plans God had for them. Look up each of the following Bible stories. Use words from the list to tell what you can learn from each one.

Word List:

listen	obey	God	trust
afraid	parents	love	

Story of Samuel (1 Samuel 3:3–9)

_____

Story of David (1 Samuel 17:38–51)

_____

Story of Jesus (Luke 2:43–51)

_____

Counting Down to Christmas

Soon it will be Christmas. It is time to prepare our hearts for His birth. We call this church season *Advent*.

Use the code to finish the Bible verse for an Advent message.

Key  a e i o u

G __ v __ H __ m th __ n __ m __

J __ s __ s, b __ c __ s __ H __ w __ ll

s __ v __ H __ s p __ pl __ fr __ m

th __ __ r s __ ns (M __ tth __ w 1:21).

Giving to Others

I will give

I will be kind to

I will share

I will show love to

The Feast of Epiphany comes after Christmas. That's when we remember the Wise Men who brought their gifts to Jesus. In this season of Advent, we prepare to give our gifts to Jesus too by showing love to those around us.

Fill in the blanks telling how you will show love each week of Advent.

I will be kind to _____

I will share _____

I will show love to _____

I will give to _____

© 2001 Carla Williams   Used by permission of Concordia Publishing House

Glory to God

At this time of year we sing songs that remind us to prepare for the birth of Christ. Listed below are the names of favorite Christmas hymns. Fill in each blank with the correct word.

"Away in a _____ "

(Manager, Manger)

"Hark the _____ Angels Sing"

(Herald, Harald)

"O, Come All Ye _____ "

(Fateful, Faithful)

"Silent _____ "

(Night, Knight)

"God Rest Ye _____ Gentlemen"

(Mary, Merry)

God's Promises

The Advent Bible readings point to the birth of Jesus. Often they do not call Him Jesus but use other names for Him. Look up these Bible passages to discover some of these names.

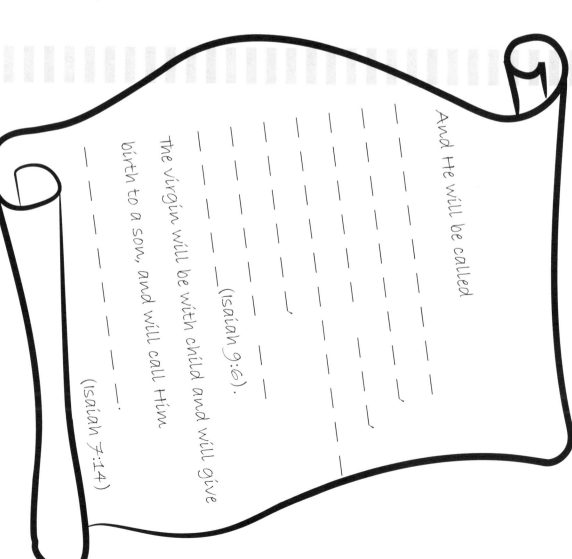

And He will be called

― ― ― ― ― ―

― ― ― ―

(Isaiah 9:6).

The virgin will be with child and will give birth to a son, and will call Him

― ― ― ― ―

― ― ― ― ―.

(Isaiah 7:14)

God used angels to tell the good news of the coming of His Son. Draw a line between the words of the angels and the person to whom the angel spoke.

Mary

Joseph

Shepherds

"Today in the town of David a Savior has been born to you; He is Christ the Lord." (Luke 2:11)

"Do not be afraid...you have found favor with God." (Luke 1:30)

"Give Him the name Jesus." (Matthew 1:21)

"Glory to God in the highest, and on earth peace to men on whom His favor rests" (Luke 2:14).

Giving to Jesus

You usually receive gifts on your birthday. Since Christmas is the day we celebrate the birth of Jesus, what gifts can you give Him? Draw a picture of something you would like to give or do for Jesus.

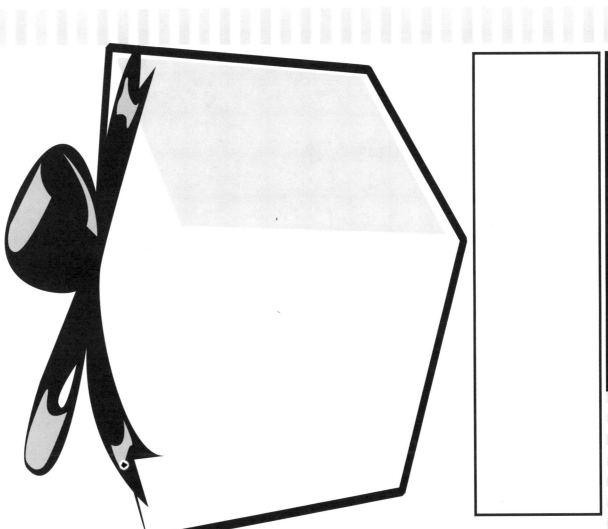

Shepherds Worship Jesus

Look carefully at the picture on this page. Then fold the page back and look at the next picture. Without peeking, can you make a list of everything that is missing.

These things are missing:

_____

_____

_____

Did you find all of them?

Christ Will Return

As Christ left this earth to be with His Father in heaven, He promised He would return to us.

Write the words on the clouds in the blanks below to find out what Jesus told us to do as we wait for His return.

your lamps

burning

and keep

ready for service

Be dressed

_____

_____

_____

(Luke 12:35).

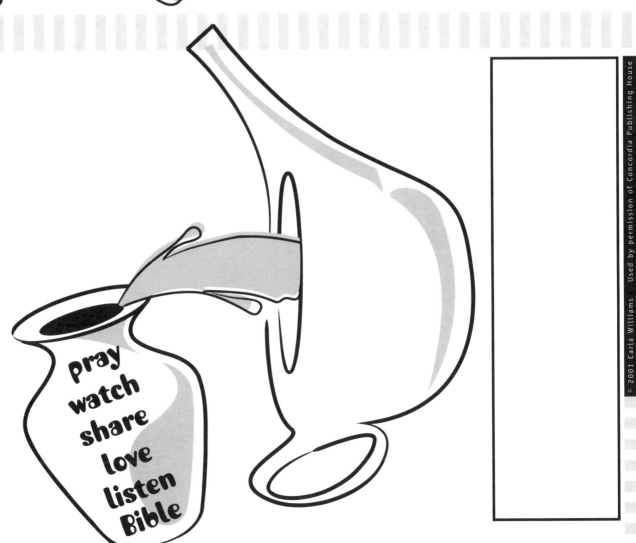

Ready for Jesus

Use words from the jug of oil to write on the lamp what you will do to be ready for Jesus when He returns.

pray
watch
share
love
listen
Bible

Keep Your Lamp Burning

Jesus told a story about **10** girls who were waiting for a wedding. **5** were foolish and **5** were wise. The **5** foolish girls took their to the wedding but they did not take any extra

oil. The **5** wise girls brought oil for their

.

It took a long time for the bridegroom to come to the wedding.

While they were waiting, the **10** girls fell asleep. At midnight the bridegroom returned. The **10** girls awoke.

The

of the **5** foolish girls ran out of oil. "Give us some of yours," they begged the **5** wise girls. "No," they replied. "If we give you some of our oil, we will not have enough. Go buy some for yourselves."

When the **5** foolish girls returned with their

filled

with oil, the door to the wedding was locked.

is like the bridegroom.

told this story to

teach us that we should be ready at all times for His return.

Select words from the jars of oil to complete the Bible verse.
(You will need to use your Bible.)

1 Thessalonians 5:16–23 suggests some ways to fill your lamp so you will be ready when Christ returns.

Be _____ always;

give _____ in all circumstances, for this is for you in Christ Jesus.

Do not put out the _____ fire; do not treat prophecies with contempt.

Hold on to the _____. Avoid every kind of _____. May God Himself, the God of _____, sanctify you through and through.

May your whole spirit, soul and body be kept _____ at the coming of our Lord Jesus Christ.

(1 Thessalonians 5:16–23)

Jar labels: peace, thanks, good, pray, blameless, spirit's, joyful, evil, God's will, Test